STATION COUNTRY III

STATION COUNTRY III

THE LAST MUSTER

Text and photography by

PHILIP HOLDEN

Hodder Moa Beckett

For station people, wherever, whenever . . .

Photographs
Front cover: Droving merinos, Central Otago
Front endpapers: Sunrise on Glenburn
Back endpapers: Sunset over the Mackenzie Country, South Canterbury
Opposite half title: Romney, Motu River Country, East Cape
Above half title and back cover: Hereford, Mackenzie Country
Title page: Bog Roy Station, on the Waitaki River, was once part
of the huge Otematata run.
Imprint page: Judy Duncan, Craigneuk, Maniototo
Opposite contents page: Romneys, Wairarapa coastline
Acknowledgements page: Gretchen and Neville Hore, Mount Alexander

ISBN 1-86958-366-3

© 1997 Text and photography Philip Holden

Published in 1997 by Hodder Moa Beckett Publishers Limited
[a member of the Hodder Headline Group]
4 Whetu Place, Mairangi Bay
Auckland, New Zealand

Edited by Alison Dench

Printed by Kyodo Printing Co. Ltd, Singapore

ACKNOWLEDGEMENTS

My heartfelt appreciation to the following people, who were either on the stations
I visited or assisted me in some way with regard to that property.

Mount Linton: Alastair McGregor, Paul McCarthy, and all
  those people I met on the property at the time of my
  visits in 1994 and 1996.
Fairlight: Jack McPherson.
Lorn Peak: Phillip Tayler.
Allandale: Angus Ross.
Upper Mataura Valley: David and Robyn Parker.
Nokomai: Brian Hore.
Galloway: Andrew Preston.
Craigneuk: John and Judy Duncan.
Otekaieke: Wendy, Mike and Tony Bayley.
Mount Alexander: Neville and Gretchen Hore.
Birchwood: Ron, Simon and Annabel Williamson.
Ben Avon: Jim and Debra Morris, Hunter Harrison,
  Kate Emmerson.
Round Hill: Grant McCrae.
Ngakaraka: Tony Pearce.
Waimoana: Bill and Lynne Thompson.
Glenburn: Gwyn and Lindy Williamson, Connie Tehuki,
  Brian Pierce, Hamish Cavanagh, Alan Schnell, Bruce
  Harding, Ian Cameron. Not forgetting a lot of station
  folk I talked with at the dog trials.
Onenui: Brian and Sally Lloyd, Butch Pardoe,
  John Hawkins, Derek Fox.

Okepuha: Phil and Gabriella Turner.
Timahanga: Jack Roberts.
Ruangarehu: Mark Williams, Rangi Haraki.
Ihungia: Tony and Gaye Hansen, Neville 'Cooch' Higgins,
  Jack Cahill, Ross Buskie, Brian McGregor, Tom Ingle,
  Julie Kilsby, Rex Chaffey. Again not forgetting a fair
  number of people I talked with at the horse sale.
Tangihau: Dean and Joanne McHardy, Faith and
  Charlie Parkes, Pat Robin, Tony Wanda, Kelly Winiata.
Ohinewairua: Richard and Mark Hayes.
Chapter 13: Stewart and Denise Bradley, Vance, Bill
  and Denise Percy.
Otairi: Doug and Ken Duncan, Simon Perry,
  Gavin Guiniven, Mark Lawry, Gary Austin.
Stonyhurst: John Douglas-Clifford.
Wharanui: Lecester and Laura Murray.
Weld Cone: Ted and Nick Webby.
The Homestead: Carol Loe.
The Muller: Steve Satterthwaite.
Flaxbourne: Cecily and Robin Petre.

To anyone I may have overlooked while working on this
  book, or, for that matter, the two previous books in
  this series, that was not my intention.

CONTENTS

Time out for the sheepdogs on Mt White.

PREFACE

It was the tail-end of the summer of '96, and I was arriving at Rock hut on Mount Linton station in western Southland. It was an agreeable day, quite different from my first visit there on the last day of winter two years earlier. That time, severe storms raging over much of the lower half of the South Island were playing havoc with the new-born lambs, a loss of $4 million to the sheep industry.

On the eastern side of the Takitimu Mountains, not far from the townships of Nightcaps and Ohai, Mount Linton station had a grand history. The McGregor family had owned the station, which now stood at 10,800 hectares, since the early part of the century; the present owner was Alastair McGregor, a tall, genial type who was also the managing director of the Mount Linton company.

Paul McCarthy, complete with Akubra hat and pleasant personality, was the general manager at the time of both of my visits. Like so many men calling the shots on the stations I had visited, Paul was nothing but the best of news. He told me the staff at the station numbered 23, large by today's standards. Four of the workforce were farm managers: they each looked after separate finishing-off properties (none larger than 517 hectares) quite apart from the main station.

On Mount Linton they were wintering 58,000 Romney ewes, 17,400 hoggets and 1300 other sheep, plus 1775 Hereford/Angus cows, 1545 other cows and 425 deer. The station was each year producing 44,000 lambs for the meat works (a short and, hopefully, happy life), 1300 head of cattle, as well as 300 Romney rams at the two Romney studs. The woolshed complex consisted of two sheds, with a total of 18 stands. At peak shearing times, with both sheds flat out, about 6000 sheep were shorn every day. Over 2000 bales of wool left the station after shearing was done.

Rock hut, some 20 kilometres from the main station complex, had bunks for 14, full cooking facilities and hot showers, and so could be considered an out-station. The term "station" originally referred to the runholder's base on a property, but in time the word came to encompass the whole kit and caboodle – buildings, land and stock. As a general rule, these days a property was considered a station if it had the capacity to run 2000 sheep. An out-station, like Rock hut, was a dwelling separate from the main station complex that might be used for only part of the year. As Paul explained at the time of my first visit, Rock hut was used for a month or so, usually a week at a time, each year. There were sheepyards and cattleyards close to hand and they weaned calves and lambs out there.

In driving rain Rock hut hadn't looked too appealing but on this day, when the weather was kind, it was an entirely different story. The out-station stood near the Wairaki River, with its waters pure enough to drink; the view was just fine and the mountain air was clear. I shared a brew in the sun with three musterers – two young men and one young woman – while the stock horses looked on.

As I look back over my travels around the country, to me these three musterers and their horses are the nameless representatives of all the musterers and horses I've encountered since I began writing about station life in 1990. And I know that, given a good horse and a spell of clear weather, I'd jump at the chance to join them as they work the high country.

Overleaf: Hawkdun Range contains the Upper Ida Burn, Otago.

WHEREVER THE
TRACK LEADS

ONE

FOLLOWING THE MATAURA

In the early autumn of 1996 I drove through Garston in northern Southland, then turned off the main highway and jolted along a metal road that more or less followed the course of the upper Mataura River.

Of all Southland rivers the Mataura was perhaps the best known. It rose on the eastern flanks of the Eyre Mountains and during its 193-kilometre journey to enter the sea at Foveaux Strait it flowed between the Garvie Mountains and the Mataura Range, crossed the Waimea plains and swept across the eastern slopes of the Hokonui Hills. It was a grand river, the Mataura.

Shortly I saw the imposing entrance way to Fairlight station on the true right of the Mataura. The old homestead, mostly screened by exotic trees, was well back from the road.

As good a way as any to begin the Fairlight story is to introduce a 33-year-old Scotsman, William Cameron, who arrived at Port Chalmers in 1855. He went into partnership with Hyde Harris of Mount Hendon station, but they were often at odds with each other and finally called it quits. Cameron decided to try his luck in the southern part of the Otago province (later Southland), which was being opened up for land development. With his sheep and cattle, and the help of several drovers, he set off across mostly virgin country and eventually came to Jacobs River (now Riverton). Here Cameron was given a very warm welcome by Captain John Howell.

Beyond the grassy plains of northern Southland rise the Eyre Mountains.

Howell was the stuff from which legends are created. He was born at Fairlight on the Sussex coast in 1809. Always of an adventurous nature, Howell was aged about 17 when he and a friend from his schooldays, William Portland, stowed away on a ship bound for Australia. It wasn't too long before they revealed themselves to the crew. Fortunately for them the captain, rather than punish them, put them to work: Howell as the officers' cabin boy, Portland in the galley.

Upon arrival in Sydney Harbour, the correct procedure would have been for the captain to hand the boys over to the proper authorities, but they had worked well and had caused not one problem. Knowing they were penniless, the good captain paid them each £2, advised them to say nothing to anyone about how they had arrived in the colony, and sent them ashore with his best wishes for their future.

John Howell found work at a huge whaling station at Twofold Bay, well south of Sydney Town. It was hard, dirty and demanding work, but young Howell was strong both mentally and physically. In time he gained a first mate's ticket and went to sea on a whaling brig under the command of Captain Lovett, a cruel taskmaster. Lovett and Howell were very often at loggerheads and the last straw came when one of the disgruntled crew voiced his grievances only to be shot dead by the captain. John Howell couldn't sign off fast enough.

The cottage Captain John Howell built for Kohi Kohi can still be seen in Riverton.

Some time later John Howell was awarded the command of the brig *Trial*, a vessel engaged in both whaling and the export of New Zealand jade to China. The *Trial* made frequent calls to the Bay of Islands and Kapiti Island, and on Kapiti Island Captain John Howell learnt much of the Maori way of life.

Meanwhile a very colourful personality had entered Howell's life. This was Johnny Jones, born in Sydney in 1809, the son of convict parents. Fiercely determined to succeed, at the age of 15 Jones worked as a sealer in New Zealand waters; later, he became a boat-man on Sydney Harbour. By the time he was 20, Jones had enough money behind him to buy shares in three whaling ships. Precisely how one so young was able to find so much money was never explained and certainly Jones, as canny as he was close-mouthed, never divulged the source of his wealth.

Jones approached John Howell, who had been a mate for a number of years, with a view to establishing a whaling base at Jacobs River in Southland. Jones would put up the required capital and Howell would oversee the establishment of the station. Captain John Howell liked the sound of this and, in accepting Jones's proposition, initiated a chain of events that would eventually see the seafaring man become a mighty runholder.

And so it was that in about 1836 Captain John Howell and 60 men came to the Maori settlement of

Aparima at Jacobs River to build one of a chain of whaling stations. Like many of his men, Captain John Howell eventually took a high-ranking Maori wife, the young, proud and graceful Kohi Kohi. With the marriage came a gift of an estimated 20,000 hectares of land.

By 1840 Howell was able to buy out Johnny Jones's share in the whaling station, but the year of 1841 brought tragedy with the death of Kohi Kohi. Two years later, he persuaded his half-brothers and sisters to leave Australia to join him in Jacobs River, and his half-sisters, Elizabeth Stevens and Ann Paulin, had the distinction of being the first Pakeha women settlers in Southland. Four years after the death of Kohi Kohi, Howell married Caroline, the half Maori daughter of Captain Broun of Codfish Island.

With a gradual decline in the whaling industry, Captain John Howell turned his attention more and more to the land. He ran sheep on his Wreys Bush run and cattle on another run at Flints Bush; later, he would build a fine homestead at Flints Bush called Eastbourne.

When in about 1856, after his disappointment at Mount Hendon, William Cameron arrived at Jacobs River with a view to taking up land in the district he found not only land – Run 133, which he called Waicola – he also found a wife in John Howell's 15-year-old daughter, the vivacious Sarah Ann. Captain Howell and his son-in-law got on famously. Cameron stocked Waicola with Merinos the captain had shipped in from Australia, but this was not Merino country: it was much too boggy.

The captain's advice to William Cameron was to look for another run, and Cameron heeded that advice. In 1858 Cameron, with his Maori guide, headed north until beyond Five Rivers he found what he was searching for. He called this run Glenquoich. The land to the north of this run was also fine-looking country, as yet unclaimed, and Cameron acquired this

run too and named it Bucurochi.

A year later, William Cameron's brother Donald took up another run in the area, Glenfalloch (later Nokomai). In 1860 William Cameron transferred Bucurochi to his father-in-law and, having sold the lease of Glenquoich, headed south again to take on the Mount Linton station, out of Ohai.

The name Bucurochi would never do for the new owner of the station and Captain John Howell renamed his run, which stretched from Glenquoich's boundary to the Mataura River, after the place of his birth: Fairlight. He made his son George manager.

By 1862 Captain John Howell had added several more Southland runs to his list of properties. Still living at Eastbourne, he visited each of his runs in turn; as time went on he became more and more captivated with Fairlight and could see a time when he would live there permanently. Meantime, George was running the place well enough.

Fairlight had a substantial workforce, usually sent up from Riverton by the captain. Apart from the expected Maoris and part-Maoris, there were two aborigines, an Irishman and a black man. Although there were sheep on Fairlight in the early 1860s, it was ostensibly a cattle run, carrying about 500 bullocks. There was a lucrative market for cattle bearing the JH brand on their ample rumps in Queenstown where, because of the discovery of gold, the population had exploded to well over 10,000.

In about 1865 George Howell, never a runholder at heart, and his wife Isabella left Fairlight and went to Riverton, where they lived in the cottage John Howell had built for Kohi Kohi. The new manager was Riverton man Fred Daniels, and he held the position for a number of years. In the late 1860s Captain Howell built a new homestead at Fairlight and it was far grander than the one at Eastbourne had ever been. In

A hard winter.

1869 the captain and his family (there were 11 children by now) came up from Eastbourne to live at Fairlight.

The early 1870s were wonderful years for sheepmen in New Zealand. The wool market boomed and Captain Howell had the sheep numbers to take full advantage of it. As the decade wore on, however, the captain, now in his sixties and no longer the fit, robust man he had been, left the running of his network of stations to his managers. He took things easy, spending time in the garden at Fairlight and hosting lavish parties and family functions.

Then in late January 1874 Captain John Howell and his wife received terrible news: two of their sons – John, 23, and Fred, 22 – had drowned. The captain, now in poor health and very often in pain, lost interest in the running of Fairlight and spent much of his time listlessly wandering about the garden. On medical advice, and at his wife's insistence, Captain John Howell retired to Riverton.

Perhaps aware that his days were numbered, Captain Howell decided to visit Sydney Town one last time. The entire Howell clan gathered in Riverton for a farewell party in his honour. The grand old man would never see his beloved Riverton again: 11 days after arriving in Sydney Town, aged 66, he died of cancer of the stomach at the residence of William Portland, his fellow stowaway of 50 years earlier.

At the time of his death Captain John Howell held title to well over 40,000 hectares of leasehold land and 400 hectares of freehold land in the Wakatipu, with stock numbers of about 40,000 sheep and 1000 cattle. Then there were his other stations, and the stock they carried, to consider. The penniless boy of years before had done himself proud in New Zealand.

Fairlight, listed at 20,000 hectares, was sold a year after the captain's death to Joseph Rodgers, who had also inherited Glenquoich from his brother William. An 1877 stock count on both of Rodgers's runs revealed they were carrying 78,000 sheep, Merino and Cheviot. The terrible winter of 1878, however, proved devastating for many an Otago and Southland runholder, and none was hit harder than Joseph Rodgers. A stock count in the spring revealed that about 40,000 sheep had perished.

It was also in 1878 that the railway came to Kingston and ended the days of bullock-drawn wagons. A small railway station with stockyards was built close to the Fairlight homestead, and records indicated there was a hotel there as well. From that point on all of the station's wool was railed to Bluff and then shipped to the home country.

The Fairlight story became sketchy from this point. The run had a string of owners until Tom Boyd gained sole possession prior to the First World War. While serving in Palestine Boyd was badly wounded, and he died in 1922. Among the trustees of Boyd's estate was William McGregor, who in 1903 had started that family's long association with Mount Linton. Needing a manager on the place McGregor, always a shrewd judge of men, appointed John McPherson in that capacity, and from the year of Tom Boyd's death until 1993 the McPhersons would be linked with one of Southland's grandest high-country runs.

At his modern home on the Frankton Arm, Jack McPherson, now in his late sixties and retired, appeared rather saddened as we talked in his sunny living room. His mood was understandable: he was recalling for me the 60 years he had spent on Fairlight station and they, like all of the golden summers of yesteryear, were never going to come back.

Fairlight, Jack told me, was pretty much overrun with rabbits when his father John had taken on the manager's job. Indeed, the rabbits had devastated

Jack McPherson.

Fairlight's once abundant grasslands, stripping the lower hills of ground cover and leaving the earth prone to erosion from wind and rain. With its stock-holding capacity greatly reduced, Fairlight was at that time carrying about 10,000 sheep and no cattle at all. An estimated 100,000 rabbits would be killed on Fairlight before the situation was reversed and tall grasses once again bent before a strong wind in the lower hill country.

Jack explained that William McGregor, soon after John McPherson had arrived at Fairlight as manager,

had offered him a third share in the run. There had been no holding John McPherson back after that and finally, in 1956, he took over the leasehold land entirely.

At the mention of the Fairlight homestead, where the seven McPherson children grew up, Jack's good-natured face lit up like a kid's at Christmas.

"That was a real family home," he said. "Great memories of growing up there."

As a five-year-old Jack went to school at Garston in a pony-drawn gig. At 12 his sister Leona drove the gig in a most accomplished fashion, with 13-year-old Margaret sitting beside her; later, Jack's younger brother Ray and younger sister Betty would make the hour-long journey too.

"A different world then," Jack mused.

To finish his schooling, Jack spent a year at the Southland Boys High School in Invercargill. I asked him how he had liked it.

Jack smiled and then chuckled. "Much to the disapproval of my father, I liked it far too much. He reckoned if we boys got too clever we wouldn't want to work on the place."

But work on the place Jack did. There were no special favours for the boss's 14-year-old son. He started on the bottom rung, as a cowboy, and there was nothing at all romantic about being a cowboy on a New Zealand station. Often as not the cowboy was an old-timer who did the menial chores: chopping wood for the homestead, milking the cow, cleaning the gigs and whatever else needed doing, the type of work a seasoned musterer or stockman would shy away from like a startled horse. Young Jack was a cowboy for a whole year.

The real highlight of the year on all of the big runs was the annual fall muster, when the sheep were brought down from their high summer range before the onset of the real snows of winter. The muster might start any time between late March and mid-April, but it had to be completed before May.

On Fairlight in those days the eight-strong mustering team and the packer (cook) still used horses to get out to the real back-country for the two-week muster. They camped at rarely used huts and mustered often as not on foot, because it was just too darn steep for even a Welsh mountain pony. Fall muster? There was nothing quite like it where Jack McPherson was concerned. All up he would be a part of 50 such musters on Fairlight, not missing one from the age of 15 until his final one in 1993, the year that the station changed hands.

Up in that rugged country where the keas gave the sheep a hard time you could often see red deer – mobs of them, a dozen, maybe 20. They were never less than a grand sight. Jack proudly indicated a stag's head on the wall, and explained that, were it not for the fall muster, he might never have seen the magnificent beast.

Almost always on a fall muster some sheep were missed. There were a number of reasons for this: the human element, the nature of the country, the fact that the sheep were spooky and scattered after several months alone, and, as always, there was the fickle weather to contend with. The straggle muster followed a fall muster and returned to the block where the sheep, called stragglers, remained.

In any event, the fall muster of 1959 on Fairlight had come and gone, but up in the heads of Eyre Creek some stragglers still ranged. It was early June when Jack and several others went to get them. Always a keen hunter, Jack had taken his rifle with him. It was while he was glassing a snowbound mountainface from the bushline – a likely spot to see sheep trapped – that he observed a mob of red deer. Thirteen stags up to their bellies in soft snow that would freeze hard once the sun retreated beyond the western peaks.

Jack refocused his fieldglasses and drew a sharp breath. One of the stags was an awesome beast with a mighty rack of antlers, points galore. He had to get it. Forgetting all about sheep, he made a long and patient stalk and triggered off a telling shot as the mob broke for the bushline. The stag turned out to be a 23-pointer that scored 363 1/2 points, Douglas Score – among the top 20 red deer heads taken in this country.

"Best red deer head I ever saw in the Eyre Mountains," Jack said as he finished the tale. Like as not, it was the best red stag that anyone had ever seen in the breathtaking country where the Mataura River had its very beginnings.

When Jack's parents retired to Frankton in the mid-1960s, Jack and Ray, both bachelors, ran the place between them. It was a satisfactory arrangement: they were mates as well as brothers and Jack had always felt very protective towards his younger (by 18 months) brother, who, although strongly built, was on constant medication for epilepsy. Over the years the Merino flock had been changed to a halfbred one and then to Romneys. The brothers slowly reintroduced cattle, Angus cows that would be mated with Shorthorn bulls to produce a more saleable calf.

With the arrival of the early 1980s the two brothers, both only in their early fifties but feeling like they were getting on in years nonetheless, decided it would make life easier if they reduced the size of the station; moreover, by selling off a substantial block of land they would be able to freehold the best of the station country. The outcome was that a 7000-hectare block of mountain country was sold to Paul Risk to become the Upper Mataura River station.

One early afternoon in August 1981, Jack told me, he and Ray took a load of fencing materials out to where the new boundary fence would be erected. As they unloaded the timber, Jack was thinking how good it was to have Mum staying with them. Good old

Mum – she was 90 now, but you'd have never guessed it. Over lunch at the homestead he and Ray had fooled around and cracked jokes like a couple of young fellas and Mum had laughed right along with them.

With the chore done, the brothers decided to shift a few sheep to another paddock. Off went Ray with his dogs; Jack would pick him up at a prearranged spot. Presently Jack arrived there, on a ridge. He looked around for Ray: he should have been there by now. Strange. Then he spotted Ray's dogs standing quietly, as though unsure, down below in the tussock. It was there that Jack found Ray lying dead in the tall grasses. Jack would always remember that his brother still had his hat on.

Jack, dreading to face his mother, returned to the homestead. It was perhaps the worst experience of his life. Sons, even more so than daughters, should never die before their mothers.

Upon selling Fairlight in 1993, like his parents before him, Jack McPherson retired to Frankton. The new owners of Captain John Howell's old run up the Mataura were the highly respected Butson family of Mount Nicholas. Another era had began, a story not yet told . . .

Beyond summer foxgloves, the Mataura River winds towards the Eyre Mountains.

TWO

DISTANT HUTS, DISTANT TIMES

In the glorious Indian summer of March 1996, the old hut stood on the western side of the Nevis River, the undulating tussocklands gradually running up behind it, bench after bench, gully after gully, until the long sweep of sun-bleached grass reached the crest of the Hector Mountains. The hut was standing there when George Tayler had taken the run on in 1960, and it looked much the same 36 years later, for the rarefied atmosphere of the high, dry valley of the Nevis River had a way of preserving things in very good order.

They were still using horses on Lorn Peak when Tayler arrived. The Lorn Peak hut, nearly five hours' ride from the homestead, had played a vital part in their big musters, which were carried out as a joint effort with John Nelson's neighbouring Kingston run. Each station had four musterers and, spread far and wide over the Hector Mountains, they brought all the sheep they could locate down to the yards at the Lorn Peak hut. Each station's sheep were identified by their coloured ear tags and, once they had been separated, Nelson took his sheep back to the flat country near Kingston and Tayler took his back over the range to where the spring runoff drained into the Mataura River.

A few weeks before I came across the old hut I visited Phillip Tayler, George's son, in the cookshop at the main station complex, and it was he who told me the history of the place. In 1970 his father purchased the Kingston

The Kingston Flyer crossing Allandale station, with the Eyre Mountains beyond.

Phillip Tayler at ease in the kitchen.

The old cookshop on Lorn Peak; the high country (behind) is Fairlight.

run to create a single station of around 11,000 hectares. After George died in 1975 Phillip and his brother Ken ran both runs between them, with Phillip in charge of Lorn Peak; in 1996 they carried 18,030 halfbred sheep.

Phillip told me that the same shearing contractor, Nigel Shirley of Lumsden, had been coming out here with his gang since 1973 and, over the years, he'd come to regard the station as a second home. Well, I thought, the old place did have a homely atmosphere about it. How many basic meals had been produced in the cookshop, I wondered? How many mugs of tea drunk? How many beers knocked back in front of the open fire?

We went outside to a lovely warm day.

"Best time of the year, the autumn," Phillip said as he angled towards the nearby woolshed.

"Either that or spring," I replied, with a sense of foreboding about the winter just around the corner.

The woolshed was what you would have expected, with the familiar smell – a mixture of greasy wool and urine and droppings – impregnated in the slatted wooden floor.

"Good old woolshed," I said, looking about me.

Phillip was pleased. "Yes, isn't it?"

As in so many woolsheds, there were names and dates carved in, or stencilled on, the sound wooden structures. The oldest date I could find was 1919 – likely the cookshop went back to about then too.

The buildings were in a very handy position, only a long rifleshot away from the Fairlight railway station and stockyards. Phillip Tayler was 12 years old when his father had taken on Lorn Peak, and at that time the railway was still in use for stock transportation between Kingston and Invercargill.

Earlier that day I had watched the Kingston Flyer tourist train chug-chugging across the tussock plains of northern Southland. A grand and, indeed, stirring sight it had made with thick black smoke belching from its chimney stack. The train was AB 778, named David McKellar after the man who was almost certainly the first European to set foot on what became Mount Nicholas station.

The modern Kingston Flyer ran from Kingston to Fairlight during the summer season, but the first Kingston Flyer was thought to have been a Yankee K class locomotive. In the mid-1880s this train was clocked on the Kingston line at a speed of 85 kilometres per hour. At the time the only freight competition was a bullock-drawn wagon. No contest. The passenger service on the Kingston Flyer north out of Invercargill was in 1936 restricted to Lumsden, and people wanting to travel on did so by bus.

The railway line here crossed Allandale station, where I'd called in and had a yarn with Angus Ross – the tall, good-looking, 32-year-old manager. Allandale, he explained, was all of 6700 hectares: it extended right into Kingston and took in country on the western side of the lake. The place, which was owned by Auckland-based Rimanui Farms, had some 3000 Romney ewes and over 200 head of cattle.

While I was talking with Angus, his three young sons had joined us. Daniel, Tony and Ben had looked typical of kids growing up on a high-country run – healthy. The boys had stood there grinning, and Dad had grinned right back at them. Angus's wife Fiona, he had told me, worked in the gallery car on the Kingston Flyer serving light refreshments and selling souvenirs.

Angus had pointed me in the direction of Allen Creek, where I had found the remnants of the walls of William Trotter's Greenvale homestead – for, like Lorn Peak, Allandale had once been part of the big station.

William Trotter, a Scotsman, came from a farming background. At the age of 23 he had gone to Australia

Angus Ross on Allandale; the high country is today's Greenvale station.

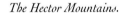

The Hector Mountains.

before being commissioned by Johnny Jones to bring 30 head of cattle on his brig *Magnet* to the recently established settlement at Waikouaiti, north of Dunedin. By the time the cattle were turned out to pasture, Jones was running around 4000 sheep and, lacking a head shepherd, he offered the position to Trotter. In accepting it, Trotter may very well have become the first head shepherd in Otago.

In 1859 Trotter went south in search of a run of his own. He found what he was looking for in Run 323, which extended from Kingston to the Mataura River and took in the broad grassy plain of the Kingston Flats, the tops of the Eyre Mountains and over the Hector Mountains clear to the Nevis River. All in all, it might have been as large as 40,000 hectares. As Captain John Howell had named his run after his place of birth, Fairlight, so did William Trotter when he called the new run Greenvale.

To stock the station, Trotter and his 20-year-old nephew, Donald Manson, brought Merino sheep and cattle from Moeraki. They travelled via the "Pigroot": to Puketoi station in the Maniototo, over Rough Ridge to Ida Valley and Galloway station, across the Molyneux (later Clutha) River at Clyde by boat or punt to Earnscleugh station, and from there over the Old Man Range to the Nevis valley, and then up and over the Hector Mountains and down to the Kingston Flats, which was luxuriant with feed.

William Trotter built his homestead complex near where the Allen Creek crossed a very lovely clearing below the Eyre Mountains. Later, in about 1871, the wooden homestead was relocated further down the flats, closer to Fairlight. An eight-stand woolshed, capable of holding 1000 Merinos, was built.

By 1867 they were running 11,200 Merino sheep and 150 head of cattle. William Trotter, who mostly resided elsewhere and could be regarded as an absentee

owner, retained his nephew as manager for quite some time. From about 1877 Trotter's oldest son, also William, appeared to have taken on this responsibility. The first William Trotter died in 1893 at the age of 78, and in about 1895 his son sold Greenvale.

By 1910 Greenvale had fallen into the hands of Alex and Archie McCaughan.

Alex McCaughan came to this country at the age of 23, and before long he found work with Frank McBride, who farmed in the Frankton district, on the eastern side of Lake Wakatipu. In time McCaughan became friends with Jack Tait, who had a gold-mining claim on the Seven Mile Creek. It meant a great deal to old Jack, who lived in a stone hut near the lakefront, that young Alex took the time to visit him and to bring out his stores from Frankton.

One day, much to McCaughan's surprise, Tait said, "I've made my pile here, Alex, and now I'm going home to Scotland."

"I will miss you, Jack."

"Aye, and I'll miss you, too." Jack Tait paused. "The claim's yours if you want it."

"Is there any gold left?"

Jack Tait laughed. "Work it and find out!"

Alex McCaughan, aware that he would never be a rich man on wages of £1 a week, quit the job he'd held for seven years and went gold mining.

Success was his! Within a few years, he had also "made his pile". Hearing that in Garston the Live and Let Live hotel and the store were up for sale, he promptly bought both of them. He remained a hotelier until 1910, when he and his brother became high-country runholders on Greenvale.

Greenvale had been through a series of short-term owners when in 1953 Bill Loft came onto the scene. In 1956 Loft's son Murray took from Greenvale a 400-hectare block near Allen Creek, and 12 years later he took

At the highest point of the "Pigroot", with the Kakanui Mountains in the background.

31

The old Lorn Peak hut, in the valley of the Nevis River.

on a further 500 hectares, which he named Allandale.

When Bill Loft sold out in 1972 Greenvale came into the hands of David and John Parker, and today David's son, Chris, aged 24, managed the now 4000-hectare property. In 1989 David and Robyn Parker also took over the Upper Mataura Valley station of 7700 hectares.

So there I was about to enter an old hut in the valley of the Nevis River that, Phillip Tayler told me, hadn't been used in over 20 years.

The interior of the hut was in dire need of a spring clean, but I'd been in far worse huts that this. Main thing was, it was dry. I looked at the sagging bunks, the wood stove, the names carved on the walls. Back in George Tayler's time the musterers of Lorn Peak and a cook had camped here, and had been joined by the crew from the Kingston run, nine men in all. It was cramped, all right: more than one man had to sleep on the floor.

William Trotter built his first homestead on Greenvale close to this lovely flat, below the Eyre Mountains. The Allen Creek crosses the far side of the flat, near the trees.

Collectively they had gathered anything from 5000 to 6000 sheep. At the end of the day a few drinks – rum, most likely – would have been drunk while the packer got on with the main meal. The men would have discussed the day's events and engaged in the easy, seldom cruel banter that goes with the territory. Outside the hut the dogs would have been tied to clumps of tussocks or to the wheels of the packer's vehicle; like me, he would have driven down the valley of the Nevis. The dogs and the horses would have been fed and the sheep, yarded, would have been quiet.

I could see the scene clearly in my mind's eye. I knew the kind of men they were because little, if anything, had changed since the early days. It was ever the same – you were darn cold saddling up under a million and one stars and darn weary when darkness fell and you unsaddled again. The life of a high-country musterer had always called for a certain breed of man – strong and resilient, the type who was quite prepared to do more than a fair day's work. Men who didn't conform to these unspoken criteria seldom lasted long in station country.

Loose gravel crunched under my tyres as I pressed on downvalley from the Lorn Peak hut. This particular back-country road would take a power of beating, both scenically and historically. I was travelling, roughly speaking, from south to north – I had joined it from a little north of Garston on State Highway 6 and the 80-kilometre journey would end on the same highway at Cromwell. This road was closed in winter because of snow.

The lower valley of the Nevis spread itself before me in the late afternoon sun: it was all browns and tans and golds, and the blue of the Nevis River, and the blue of the sky, and a few wispy puffs of clouds. I was enchanted by it all. Beyond the winding band of the river, to the east, was the long, narrow Nevis block on Nokomai, the station owned by the Hore family since 1950.

Ben Nevis station buildings in the lower valley of the Nevis.

I paused at the Ben Nevis station to look over the remains of a building on the side of the road, ran my hands over the splintered woodwork of an old wagon. There was plenty of hard evidence of gold diggings from bygone times: crumbling stone dwellings, heaps of rubble, scarred flats. They still sought gold in the Nevis and they still found payable quantities of it too.

A small bridge took me across to the true right of the river; here the road started to climb quickly out of the wide, high valley. A bunch of Herefords ranged rocky habitat over near an old homestead on Craigroy station. There would be a story to tell there, too – there always was.

The road levelled out and I lurched over the highest spot and then stopped: the view was extensive and altogether awe-inspiring. I clambered out to hear skylarks and pipits singing. I was more or less overlooking Cromwell and Lake Dunstan to the north; in the distance I could make out the sun-hazed mountains that surrounded Lakes Wanaka and Hawea, part of the huge watershed of the Clutha River.

Much of the land I could see had once been part of the McLeans' massive Morven Hills station, which, like the present-day run of the same name, extended to the Lindis Pass country. The valley was enclosed on its western side by the Pisa Range and in the east by the Dunstan Mountains. Today's Bendigo and Northburn stations, once part of the McLeans' kingdom of grass, ran back to the many-ridged Dunstan Mountains. There were other stations even closer: Cairnmuir and Kawarau.

In fact, there were stations whichever way I happened to look. To the east, for instance, beyond the Old Man Range, was Earnscleugh; further back, across an unseen Clutha and below the Knobby Range aglow in the late sun, was the little-known Riverside station. It was country to fire one's imagination, all right.

Looking across the Nevis River flats to Nokomai station and the Old and New Roaring Lion huts.

THREE

THE FIRST MERINOS IN CENTRAL OTAGO

My companion, tall and broad-shouldered, pointed out from the cab of the four-wheel-drive vehicle distant sheep amidst the tall grasses that flourished here on the plateau-like Raggedy Range in Central Otago. They were Merinos, ewes and lambs, and they had been there since September – nearly four months earlier – and would remain so until early March.

We drove closer and they ran through the native tussocks.

"They're great-looking sheep," I said.

"Yeah, they do real well up here." Andrew Preston, the 33-year-old owner of Galloway station, was running some 9000 such sheep on 11,000 hectares.

This was also summer range for cattle – Herefords, mainly, and in top condition too. I noticed that there were some obviously crossbred animals mixed in with the brown-and-white bunch and Andrew explained that they'd used a Charolais bull over a Hereford cow to obtain the crossbred stock. The big crossbred calves were in fine fettle and would, Andrew added, command a premium price when they went to market.

More sheep came in view. They huddled together in the open, head to head in little bunches, or camped alone in weather-eroded hollows under outcrops of rock. They weren't finding much shade from the searing sun, but this was Merino country and they were well used to it.

Andrew Preston on Galloway station.

36

The Manuherikia River in the icy grip of winter.

Merino country? Why, it had never been anything but that on Galloway station.

Among the passengers to arrive in Dunedin in October 1857 on the 240-tonne ship the *Thomas and Henry* were two young Scotsmen, Watson and Alexander Shennan. Watson, 23, was seven years older than his brother and very much the driving force behind their move to the far side of the world. His intention was to take up land for raising sheep somewhere in the hinterland of the province of Otago.

Two things soon became apparent to the Shennan brothers: firstly, there were no horses to be had anywhere in Dunedin and, secondly, the region they were interested in was still being explored and surveyed by the chief surveyor for the province, John Turnbull Thomson.

As far as the horses went, they would have to wait for a shipment from Australia in December. And as far as the map went, they would have to make do with one

drawn by a Maori many years before. This map, although quite detailed, carried only one name: the Manuherikia River. The river appeared to lie beyond several ranges of hills or mountains, a round trip of perhaps several weeks.

In early December they bought two riding hacks and a packhorse and set off from the Tokomairiro Plain (in the vicinity of Milton) towards the hinterland. The old map they had copied proved accurate and presently they came, in fine weather, to the northern end of the Knobby Range. Here they gazed across today's Alexandra to the Manuherikia valley.

They camped that night on the banks of the Manuherikia and next day went upriver. Only a few weeks previously Thomson and his two assistants had ridden down the same valley to where it joined the Clutha and found "superior grasses near the joining of the rivers". The brothers explored the valley as far north as Blackstone Hill and, at that point, crossed the

Raggedy Range to come to the very lovely Ida Valley. This too was both well grassed and well watered. They then surmounted Rough Ridge and from there they looked upon the vast Maniototo Plain.

Low on supplies and having seen the land they wanted to make a claim for, they started back to Dunedin. Watson Shennan later wrote, "I kept on the high country for a long distance, but on the high ground it was difficult to find good camping places, so I tried the lower flats. But this was a mistake, for swampy ground was met with and was very unpleasant for camping. It was a most uncomfortable situation – not a stick to boil the billy and nothing but big snow tussocks for the horses to eat." They called the area Dismal Swamp.

To gain land in early 1858 required an application to the Waste Land Board and the Shennan brothers duly applied. They were granted a depasturing licence for two blocks of land – a total of 65,000 hectares – in the valley of the Manuherikia River. The larger of these two blocks, to the east of the river, they called Galloway after their birthplace. The smaller block was very much bounded by water – the Molyneux River, Chatto Creek and the Manuherikia – and they named it Moutere, which means "island".

In March 1858 the brothers Shennan and their hired help rode into the six-year-old settlement of Balclutha, on the banks of the lower reaches of Clutha River. They purchased an unknown number of Merino sheep from a local runholder; all they had to do now was get them to the Manuherikia.

The trip lasted about six weeks. They had decided to cross the Lammerlaw Range, a rather confusing, many-ridged system of tussock-clad hills rising to over 1000 metres, but even before they reached the foothills they faced days of torrential rain. So boggy were the conditions that their dray proved quite useless, and it was sent back to Balclutha to be replaced with sledges.

Late evening on the Maniototo Plain, with Rough Ridge on the skyline.

The Galloway homestead is as sound today as it was in 1865.

Two weeks were lost before the journey progressed.

In 1910 Watson Shennan published a brief account of this droving trip in the *Tapanui Courier*. We take it up with the arrival of the sledges:

The sheep journeyed on, with provisions carried on pack horses, but progress was very slow on account of the rough nature of the country. They had to go over the highest part of the Lammerlaws, when one of the severest snowstorms imaginable caught them. What happened during the following three or four weeks would take more time and space to describe than the writer can afford. I will only say that I do not think it possible to experience greater hardship and live – especially that suffered by the party with the sheep; and having to change the dray for sledges caused much of the trouble.

The sheep (with my brother in charge) and the bullock teams, personally driven, got separated some forty miles [65 kilometres] by a mountain. The Lammerlaws were covered with snow, from four to thirty feet [1.25 to 9 metres] deep. The teams could not face this, and there was no way round. The party with the sheep I knew would be getting short of provisions, and that made me very anxious, as it was impossible to say what had happened to them if caught in the snow. It was necessary to push on, and I made two attempts, both times getting a long way up the mountain; but was driven back to lower ground by fresh snowstorms. The third try was successful. Where the snow was deep it got frozen hard, and carried the bullocks and sledges, so my charge managed to get over. My party had nothing hot to eat or drink for three days, and the bullocks were not out of the yokes for the same time, and had hardly any food.

When I picked up the party with the sheep in Ida Valley, they were out of provisions, and had only mutton to eat for some days, and had lost a man and horse. The missing man had been sent back to bring up some stores that had been left behind, but he did not find the provisions and lost himself. After three days' search my brother managed to pick him up. He had had very little food, and I have never seen a man so hungry as he was; but we restricted him to small quantities of food for some days. The party with the sheep had a terrible experience in the snow, and for over a week the mob could not be moved. They were practically under the snow, and were in deep snow for three weeks. The horses had to be moved from one big snow tussock to another, that being the only food they could get. The party could only find enough sticks to boil the billy and cook a chop; not sufficient for a fire to warm them. A journey to the South Pole is nothing to a trip like that.

But, whatever the hardships, it was all worth it when they reached the Manuherikia and turned out their Merinos to graze where none had ever foraged before.

Like many other early sheepmen in this country they were faced with a serious problem: wild dogs. These were the truly feral descendants of Maori dogs. Mostly tan in colour, they were about the size of a collie, but

The Lammerlaw Range.

41

Out on the Galloway run.

with shorter legs, a thick woolly coat, alert ears and sharp features. They did not bark but, rather, made a long, mournful, dingo-like call. They survived mostly on native birds, which were far more abundant then because the country was considerably more forested.

In his report of 2 November 1858, William Pinkerton, a sheep inspector in Otago (southern district), would write:

The great present evil is wild dogs. The losses from this cause are enormous, and the number of sheep scattered by them is very great. I would strongly recommend everyone – particularly during the summer months – to bring their sheep home every night to camp near the shepherd's hut, or surround them with poisoned baits, which ought to be taken up every morning. Let the shepherd be well provided with dogs and remain with his sheep during the day.

Like other runholders, the Shennans tried shooting as a means of eliminating the wild dogs, but the dogs proved elusive. Poison was not the answer: some of their own dogs might take the bait, and in a land lacking fences a good sheepdog was too valuable to lose. The solution proved to be large packs of stag-hounds brought from Australia. They were used throughout the region to systematically hunt down, and destroy, the sheep-killers. Eventually the true feral dog became extinct.

Shearing appeared to have been first carried out on Galloway in late 1858. The shearers were paid 15 shillings a day and were each allotted three glasses of rum, presumably at the end of the day. The transportation of the clip to the coast at Waikouaiti, 200 kilometres away, was Watson's responsibility. He took two bales at a time on a bullock-drawn sledge; on the return trip he brought station supplies.

It was said that it took Watson Shennan most of the summer to transport all of Galloway's wool to the coast. At two bales per trip that was hardly surprising. Later, when roading improved, bullock-drawn drays capable of carrying a much bigger load were used on Galloway.

The Shennans sought constantly to improve the standard of their flock. They did so by importing long-wool sheep from Scotland (in 1859 and 1861), and by introducing new blood from the North Island, where the Merino breed, prone to footrot, was by and large considered a failure.

Early in 1860 they disposed of the Galloway run and concentrated their efforts on Moutere. The new owner of Galloway was William Low (who also owned Cairnhill station). In the September of that year Low, pressed for funds, formed a partnership in both of these properties with land baron Robert Campbell.

By all accounts Low, an Englishman, was easy to work for. By the rather strict standards of those times – when Jack was never as good as his master – he was a very lenient employer. With other business interests to pursue Low, as often as not, was absent from Galloway, and he put the day-to-day running of the place in the hands of a manager. But when Low was at the station he liked nothing more than being on horseback, out on the run, checking the condition of the sheep and the pasture.

One hot summer's day found Low following one of the station's boundaries, unfenced but marked with piles of rocks at regular intervals along, for instance, an obvious ridge. Presently he spotted a saddled horse tied to a patch of scrub; nearby, a roughly dressed man lay on his back, dozing. Low was pretty sure this was the new man on the place, a boundary keeper or rider he had not met. Such men lived in remote stone huts or, at times, under canvas.

The boundary keeper looked up as Low drew rein and looked down at him; he made no move to get up or to speak. To test his general knowledge of the country, Low asked which was the way to Black's run (at Lauder). The boundary keeper indicated the general direction by casually stabbing a toe. Shaking his head, Low said, "Is that all the courtesy you can show a traveller?" The man, still stretched out on the ground, did not reply. Later that boundary keeper was told by the manager just who it was who'd asked him the way to Black's run and added that he, the boundary keeper, was very lucky that he still had a job.

On another occasion, Low entered a billiards saloon in Alexandra. Low watched the players for a time; one of them was very skilled and Low asked him who he was. The man explained that he was one of Low's boundary keepers.

"And this, I suppose, is your boundary?" Low was said to have replied.

That particular boundary keeper could have well expected his marching orders but he too retained his position on Galloway, thanks to Low's leniency and his sense of humour.

On Moutere, always looking for ways to improve the flock, Watson Shennan decided to import purebred Merinos from Europe. It was decided that 21-year-old Alexander, who had never been as robust as his brother, would attend to the matter personally. It was hoped that the sea voyage of around three months would improve his poor health, which was caused, they believed, by the hardships of pioneer life at a vulnerable age.

Alexander appeared to have arrived in Europe in the spring of 1861. From the King of Prussia's famed

Potsdam Stud he obtained 15 rams and 27 ewes, and from England he acquired two Leicester rams. Alexander did not, however, return to New Zealand; instead he enrolled as a medical student at Edinburgh University. Presumably he had had more than enough of raising sheep in Otago.

In any event, Watson Shennan's prized stud Merinos, purchased at a cost of £2000, were, under the supervision of Scotsman James Beattie, shipped to New Zealand on the *Oliver Cromwell*. They arrived at Port Chalmers on 7 April 1862, where they were transferred to a smaller vessel and taken to Waikouaiti. It was high tide when they arrived and Beattie was dismayed to discover there was no wharf. This was not a cause for concern for the old hands, however: strong Maori backs carried both sheep and Beattie safely ashore, a unique introduction to the young colony for a hardy young Scotsman and the first purebred stud Merinos imported into Otago.

It was in the following year that Watson Shennan received devastating news. Alexander had died of rheumatic fever. Watson's grief was profound. He lost his appetite for life in the colony and before long sold up and returned to Scotland. In September 1869, however, he would be back in New Zealand as the new owner of Puketoi station in the Maniototo; it was here that his Merino stud gained a reputation that spread around the world.

At Galloway in 1865 a new homestead was built to replace the clay-walled, flax-roofed dwelling the Shennans had built and which had been flooded out several times when the Manuherikia broke its banks. The design of this homestead had been the lot of a willing Mrs Low, the fourth daughter of Dr Andrew Buchanan of Dunedin. She had drawn plans for a 12-roomed homestead with stone walls 60 centimetres thick and cob partitions; the ceilings would not be too high, the main corridor would be narrow. Above all it would be a family home, warm in winter, cool in summer. Mrs Low planned well: 130 years later the homestead still stood, along with the singlemen's quarters, stables and chaff house, as sound as ever.

At this point William Gilbert Rees, a runholding legend known as King Wakatip, made an appearance in the Galloway story. After a series of disappointments, including having his lease on one block cancelled when the area was declared a goldfield, Rees sought employment as a station manager. In 1867 he was offered the manager's position on Galloway, and he was more than pleased to accept it; he remained there until 1872.

William Low's association with Galloway came to an end in 1878 when he sold his shares in the property to Robert Campbell. In 1883 Campbell engaged a manager called R. Gunion, who remained there for 13 years. By now the days of the shearers' allocation of three glasses of rum a day were history, as can be seen from the strict regulations that existed during Gunion's time:

Any shearer who shall be drunk during engagement or who shall bring intoxicating liquors on to the station or who shall wilfully or persistently infringe any provision or who shall be absent without permission or just cause from the shed during working hours shall be liable to dismissal and to forfeit by way of liquidated penalty five shillings for each hundred sheep shorn by him to be deducted and retained from the amount due to him at the time of settlement.

When Gunion moved on in 1896, Alex Gunn, the father of Davy Gunn of the Hollyford, became the new manager of Galloway. He remained until the station was subdivided in 1916–17.

So the mighty Galloway was no more. The main block was reduced to 11,500 hectares; today's Matangi, Riverside, Little Valley, The Crawfords, Mount Campbell and Goulburn were once part of the run taken up by the Shennans.

A short time after the subdivision the main Galloway block was secured by the Spain family of Earnscleugh station and it remained in their hands until 1929, when Harold Preston purchased it. The Preston family, who came from England originally, had made their mark farming in the Oamaru district.

When Harold died in 1962 his son Ken became the runholder. Andrew Preston was thrust into that role in 1984 when Ken died at the age of 59. The new man on Galloway was just 21 years old, but youth was never a barrier on that station: Watson Shennan was only 23 and his brother still a teenager when they drew rein on the northern end of the Knobby Range and saw the beautiful valley of the Manuherikia spread out before them.

The old Rabbit Board hut on Goulburn.

SHEARING AT GALLOWAY STATION

The shearing time has come again,
The cook is in the galley,
The learners here all mean to try
and beat the ringer's tally.

We're rather short of shearers yet,
We only have the two,
But when they're in the humour
They can shove out quite a few.

We've a slim wee chap works on the board,
He picks up all the fleeces,
By the time they reach the table
They're mostly all in pieces.

He's a ball of muscle most days,
He's as fit as any flea,
Just watch him jump to tar the place
Where the hind leg used to be.

There's two chaps at the table,
With their pinafores and shoes
They're just exactly what they look –
Two worn-out cockatoos.

There's a part-time presser on the job
We'll mention in this rhyme,
He's a cockatoo from down the road
But he's not here all the time.

There's a shepherd works around the shed,
He's always in for lunch,
He's got a pack of mustering dogs
That seem a handy bunch.

Here comes the boss, we know his step,
"Well, boys, the sheep are tough,
You're shoving out the tallies
But you're getting mighty rough.

"You squeal for higher wages
And you'd take it every one,
And yet you're sending half my wool
Out upon the run."

And when the smoko comes along
They sit round on the bales,
They entertain each other
Telling funny tales.

The tales are very funny
When you hear them tell them right,
There's other ones quite good to hear
That you really wouldn't write.

The boss says in his pleasant way
As he gives a little cough,
"My sheep won't get rheumatics
If you take the stockings off."

I've seen some woolsheds in my time
And I've worked in quite a few,
But Galloway seems different –
Each man's a cockatoo.

Anonymous

And so on a very warm midsummer's afternoon in 1996, Andrew Preston and I were on the crest of the Raggedy Range and I thought to myself the Merinos that ran through the grasses before us were of good enough quality to have pleased even the likes of Watson Shennan.

As we pressed on, I couldn't help but think about the past: of the valley of the Manuherikia untouched, the Shennans' arrival on horseback, of their epic droving trip across the snowy Lammerlaw Range, of young Watson's taking wool to the coast over Rough Ridge, two bales per trip, and what he would have made of today's transportation. I imagined the great mobs of sheep that had ranged the station before it was subdivided, as well as the rabbits in their untold numbers. I formed a mental picture of William Rees, a fellow Welshman, who had ridden across this land in the 15 years he was the manager. And I thought of the young Davy Gunn crossing this land on horseback. All here, on Galloway.

Breaking into my thoughts, Andrew pointed out David Small's Goulburn station to the north. I mentioned that I'd been on Goulburn late the previous winter, when I'd driven in to see the Upper Manorburn dam. On a high plateau – even higher than here – I'd spotted an old Rabbit Board hut and taken the time to check it out. The one-roomed dwelling was full of bird droppings; it'd been a darn long time since a rabbiter, or anyone else for that matter, had boiled a billy in there.

"I love it here, y'know," Andrew suddenly said with feeling. "I mean, where else could you get" – he made a gesture that took in the St Bathans and Hawkdun Ranges, the Remarkables and the Old Man Range – "a view like this?"

Andrew Preston had spent all of his life here. He would have seen this same view countless times and yet he hadn't become complacent about it. I liked him a whole lot for that.

Goulburn station's high country.

FOUR

FROM ONE EXTREME TO ANOTHER

"And this," Wendy Bayley said in her pleasant, well-modulated voice, "is the cave where Dansey lived when he first came here."

She stepped back a little and indicated that I should go ahead of her. I stooped to pass through a narrow opening in the limestone cliff-face and entered an almost circular cavern, a roomy chamber. It was as dry in there as old roo bones in a central Australian desert.

"In Robert Campbell's time," Wendy went on in much amplified tones, "they kept blocks of ice here in winter."

Outside again in the grey drizzle, Wendy drew my attention to a stone cottage. William Dansey had built the one-roomed dwelling hard against the cliff-face soon after he had taken on Otekaieke in 1857; the cave

must have had its limitations. "The thatch roof isn't original," Wendy pointed out.

Someone in recent times had covered with thatch the part of the roof that could be seen from the front in the mistaken belief that this was what Dansey had used in the first place. Wrong. The corrugated-iron sheeting they had removed, but which covered the part of the roof that could not be seen, was almost certainly Dansey's choice.

Within an easy stroll of the cave and the stone cottage was Wendy and Mike Bayley's two-storeyed homestead, the same one that had been home for Dansey and his wife in 1861. Also nearby was Robert Campbell's 30-room mansion dating to 1876.

Approaching Dansey Pass from the Maniototo side.

Wendy Bayley vanished in the direction of her 135-year-old home and I had a closer look at the cave. It was at the other end of the scale from Campbell's mansion: the cave was as basic a habitation as you could get, while a many-roomed mansion on a working sheep station was simply ostentatious. It was truly a case of one extreme to another on arguably the most famous old station in the big valley of the Waitaki River.

Otekaieke was first taken up in 1854 by Samuel Helier Pike, possibly in partnership with a brother. Pike ran cattle on his run but did not appear to have lived there on a regular basis. Unlike sheep, cattle could be pretty much left to fend for themselves.

In December of the same year, William Heywood Dansey arrived at Port Chalmers on board the *Pudsey Dawson*. The well-educated but adventurous 24-year-old son of a Church of England clergyman was keen to take up land in the young colony and, while not rich by the standards of the day, was in the financial position to do something about it.

In Dunedin Dansey purchased a horse and set out to explore the region, and when he came to the Waitaki valley he liked what he saw. An altogether friendly and genial type, Dansey quickly made friends with the Pike brothers on Otekaieke station as well as with Harrie Carr Robison, another young Englishman determined to make it in New Zealand.

Dansey did not rush things; sensibly, he elected to familiarise himself with the country before making a decision about taking up land. At this time, of course, very little was known about Central Otago – the

Robert Campbell's mansion.

Shennan brothers, for instance, were still in Scotland. Dansey did know, however, about the Maniototo, the land which lay beyond the high peaks and contained the Waitaki watershed. The area had been described by Charles Kettle, the then official surveyor for the colony, in 1847 as "an immense extent of country stretching away into the interior of the island . . . 700,000 acres [280,000 hectares] of low undulating grassy downs . . . offering every inducement for the depasturing of sheep and cattle . . ."

Dansey was more than eager to see the Maniototo for himself, but the difficulties in getting there provided food for much thought. One might surmount the St Marys Range, within Otekaieke's far-flung and ill-defined southern boundaries, but the ascent was dangerous for men and impossible for packhorses or mules. Dansey, looking for other options, turned to an old Maori identity for information. Yes, the man said, there was an easier route, one that his people had used for a very long time. Dansey pressed him further and the Maori drew a rough map.

When Dansey made known his intention to find a route from the Waitaki valley to the Maniototo he was not short of volunteers to go with him. In 1855 Dansey, Harrie Carr Robison, Charles Hopkinson (a runholder from Shag Valley) and a man called Morley set off on their grand adventure. They went on foot, with a donkey and mule to carry their equipment and supplies.

From today's Duntroon they headed inland, following the course of the Maerewhenua River. It was slow going – the river banks were choked with heavy scrub – and Dansey was pleased they had decided against taking saddle horses with them.

Presently they came to a fork in the river. They took the right branch, and this eventually brought them to a distinct saddle. On one side, to the south, rose the Kakanui Mountains, on the northern side rose the St Marys Range. It was spectacular country; they had seen none better. They camped below the saddle, which, given time, would become known as Dansey Pass.

Overnight their donkey wandered off into one of the many gullies which formed the headwaters of the Kye Burn and the explorers searched for it in vain. Carrying their swags, they went on without it, criss-crossing the ever-growing Kye Burn, down towards a high and windswept plain that appeared to stretch forever. They had reached the Maniototo. In years to come Danseys Pass would be the high point in a much-used dray and stock track linking the Waitaki valley with Central Otago.

At Omarama this statue, sculptured by Bill Adams in 1994, was erected as a tribute to Merino sheep.

In May 1856 Dansey, still not yet a runholder, was staying with the Pikes when two bearded strangers arrived at Otekaieke station. Edmund Davidson and his employee W.H.S. Roberts were en route from Nelson to the Waimea plains north of Invercargill, where Davidson had acquired a run. In later life Roberts became a noted historian, drawing from the diary he religiously kept. He did not record what accommodation the Pikes lived in – the cave, under canvas, or something of both – but he was very interested in how they ground flour.

There were no men or servants on the station so we had to cook for ourselves and also grind the wheat to make scones. Mr Pike had a box hand-mill which ground the wheat and separated the flour into firsts, seconds and bran. It was pretty hard work turning it but was a great improvement on the general runs of mills which did not even take the coarsest of the bran out but left it wholemeal in reality.

The men stayed for a while at Otekaieke station, and Dansey hit it off extremely well with both of them. Davidson promised to stay in touch and let Dansey know if there was any possibility of his taking on a run in the Waimea plains.

Davidson was true to his word and wrote to Dansey explaining that there were plenty of runs not yet taken and suggesting he come down and see for himself. Dansey considered that. New country! What had he got to lose? Nothing, absolutely nothing!

Dansey headed south with the express intention of becoming a runholder in the Waimea plains. In January 1857 he arrived at Davidson's station Titipua with 108

The Otekaieke homestead dates to the early 1860s.

head of cattle, driven with the assistance of two men. Davidson's sheep had not yet arrived, so Dansey left his cattle to graze on Titipua while he went to Dunedin to secure a pastoral lease. W.H.S. Roberts wrote in his diary: "Mr Dansey had left the calf of one of the cows at Chubbin's, so we yarded the cow and milked her every day for many weeks. Oh what a treat we thought the milk! A luxury we had not enjoyed for months!"

Dansey secured the lease for Run 181 and became a real runholder at last. His lease was for 14 years, at a yearly fee of £6. At about this time Dansey, much to his dismay, heard that Pike had sold Otekaieke to John Parkin Taylor. What he would have given to own that station!

As fate would have it, the new owner decided to turn over Otekaieke very quickly and word of this reached Dansey while he was still in Dunedin on business. Otekaieke, then, might not be a lost cause. Dansey acted smartly and negotiated to buy Otekaieke, using Run 181 as part payment.

In November 1857 Roberts was hired by Taylor to take what had been Dansey's cattle to his run on the Waiau. As for Run 181, it was known first as The Elbow, and later as Castle Rock. Located near today's Lumsden, Castle Rock would become one of the best-known stations in all of Southland.

On Otekaieke Dansey set to with a will. To start with he lived in the cave, that bone-dry chamber used for centuries by the moa-hunters as they journeyed up and down the Waitaki. One meaning of the word Otekaieke was "the place of a house or shelter" and this may well have referred to the cave.

Dansey married, perhaps about the time he built his cottage. On a slope behind the cottage he would dig two small graves to hold the bodies of his children, who ate the poisonous black berries of deadly nightshade.

In 1858 Dansey's friend Harrie Carr Robison also became a Waitaki runholder, when he took on Omarama station from Parson Andrews, who'd secured it two years previously. It was then in excess of 56,000 hectares. For Robison, who before coming to New Zealand had been a bank clerk, Omarama station was heaven sent.

Also in 1858 Kyeburn station was established in the Maniototo by Barton and McMasters. Nearly 50,000 hectares in size, Kyeburn adjoined Otekaieke station at Danseys Pass. Not long after the land was taken up, a Kyeburn mustering gang came across a most unusual sight in one of the gullies below the pass: the donkey that had strayed from Dansey's party a few years previously. The donkey, while quite pleased to make contact with humans again, seemed none the worse for its lonely, high-altitude existence.

Financially, things went very well for Dansey on Otekaieke. By 1859 he was running over 5000 sheep and two years later he commissioned James Dunn and James May to build a substantial homestead. They used blocks quarried from the same cliff-face Dansey had built his cottage from. The gracious two-storeyed homestead had walls 60 centimetres thick, making it cool in summer and warm in winter. The fine cookshop and shearers' quarters near the homestead and the big woolshed dated to this period too.

On the run, Dansey's sheep increased in numbers very nicely. In 1862 Otekaieke was carrying in excess of 12,000 Merinos and a flock of English Leicester sheep which had been brought from England and landed at Oamaru at a cost of £14 pounds a head. By this time he had extended the station's eastern boundary to the Maerewhenua River.

The cookshop and shearers' quarters were built in the late 1850s.

In those days such big runs as Otekaieke and Kyeburn lacked boundary fences and both stations had boundary riders on the payroll. The stations gave their sheep an easy time of it over summer, letting them range, and the Merinos, never sedentary creatures, wandered far and wide. The sheep from Dansey's run would end up on Kyeburn and vice versa, and at mustering time such sheep were kept in a special pen near Danseys Pass before being handed back to their rightful owners. This type of thing went on for years.

Otekaieke became known as a top station to work on. Dansey won the respect of those he employed because he was not afraid to pitch in and give every task his best shot. He was also generous to a fault and no one who turned up at the station was refused a bed for the night or a meal to fill the stomach. Young Scotsman James Strachan, who might have jumped his ship at Port Chalmers, took to the road with a swag in this period and recorded his travels in his diary:

I went to Otekaieke and spent a comfortable night. Mr Dansey's was considered the best "shop" to stay at on the Waitaki. It was called the "Waitaki Hotel". Unfortunately for him he was too good and when the diggins broke out the hard-ups nearly ate him out of house and home. He was too good a sort was Mr Dansey.

In the mid-1860s the main talk among runholders in New Zealand was the deteriorating price for wool. It was the right time for someone with capital to move in and buy up stations that might not otherwise have come on the market. Such a man was Robert Campbell. Born in England in 1843, Campbell came from an extremely wealthy and influential family. Following his education, in about 1863 young Robert came out to New Zealand at the instigation of his father with the prime objective of taking up land on a grand scale.

In their whistle-stop tour of much of the lower part of the South Island, Campbell and his well-informed associates had visited Otekaieke. They liked what they saw: the buildings were excellent, the homestead would make an ideal manager's residence, the sheep were first-rate and Dansey himself was a jolly good fellow. There were other stations in the Waitaki watershed that appealed to Campbell, but top of the list was Otekaieke.

There was no record to say just how much Dansey was offered to sell Otekaieke but, whatever it was, he gladly accepted. He moved to Oamaru, where he became the first man in the town to receive the old age pension. He died in Taranaki in 1907.

Within a year, Campbell had for £36,000 snapped up Benmore station, north of Omarama. Benmore, taken up by Alexander McMurdo in 1857, was the second run (after Omarama) taken up in the Omarama district. It took in all of the land between the Ahuriri and Ohau Rivers and, at about 128,000 hectares, was of breathtaking size. What was more, most of the Benmore country could hold sheep, so its potential was almost unlimited.

In 1869, with wool prices falling even lower, for £40,000 Campbell acquired Station Peak, on the north side of the Waitaki River in South Canterbury. With Station Peak came 41,000 sheep, 13,500 lambs, 50 cattle and 16 horses. The three stations – Otekaieke, Benmore and Station Peak – would be run in conjunction with each other.

On Benmore Robert Campbell, all of 23 years old, made sweeping changes, and a new homestead, woolshed and yards were built. From Germany he imported 70 purebred Merino rams, and from Australia a considerably larger number of Merino ewes. About 20 men were regulars; at shearing time as many as 100 men were on the place. And always at the helm was a good manager, for Campbell, with other stations to consider and various business ventures that demanded his time, was as dependent in that regard as any absentee owner.

Stables and coach house stand near Robert Campbell's mansion.

Of all the stations he would own, Robert Campbell appeared to have best liked Otekaieke. Indeed, he would in time become known as "Campbell of Otekaieke". It did not displease him. At Otekaieke he had built a huge, Scottish-style baronial mansion. Near the mansion, and also dating to 1876, were the stables and coach house, complete with Romanesque arches and built around a central courtyard. It was all very grand, and all very much misplaced. Robert Campbell was an English gentleman well removed from everyday station life.

Campbell was more interested in the running of his dozen or more stations on a broader company level. He became interested in local affairs: he was president of the Waitaki County Council, served on the board of governors of the Waitaki Boys High School and even

The Ahuriri Bluffs, one of Robert Campbell's favourite quail hunting spots.

Otekaieke cattle out near Danseys Pass.

went to Parliament, firstly in the House of Representatives and later the Legislative Council.

Robert Campbell was a good man to work for and he and his wife Emma (daughter of English-born Australian explorer Joseph Hawdon) were wonderful hosts at the many functions held at Otekaieke. Campbell was no stuffed shirt: he loved his racehorses and he greatly enjoyed hunting upland gamebirds.

Perhaps more than anything Robert Campbell was proud of his ability to handle a team of horses, and he was regarded as a fine reinsman. Over the Christmas period one year a large picnic was held on Benmore and most of the people who worked on the other Campbell runs attended it. The manager on Benmore, Scotsman Tom Middleton, was not one to belittle his own ability when it came to handling a team of horses, and Campbell challenged him to a race. They would each drive a six-horse team for a distance of about a mile.

Middleton agreed to the contest but, when he saw Campbell's team, he protested that they were much better than the horses he would be using. To make up for it, Campbell offered Middleton a start of about a quarter of a mile. Fancying his chances, Middleton took off along the coach road to the sounds of cheering from the onlookers. Campbell contained his straining team until his manager was the required distance ahead of him and then urged them on. An even bigger cheer rang out.

Campbell did indeed have the better, faster team, and soon he was closing the gap. Then he was moving right up to Middleton, the dust swirling in his face, blinding his vision, the coach road too narrow to overtake, and Middleton not at all inclined to move over. Campbell pulled his team off the road to jolt across the uneven, tussocky land, to draw level with Middleton, to pull ahead of him, to cut back suddenly so that he was in front and Middleton was choking on his dust. Robert Campbell finished the race a good team's length in front of his manager.

In 1889, at the comparatively young age of 46, the Hon. Robert Campbell died. His enormous wealth would be later displayed for all to see in a bequest by Mrs Emma Campbell which resulted in a large Anglican vicarage being built in Kurow and, at the other end of the parish, the imposing St Martin's Church in Duntroon. The township of Duntroon had taken the name of a Campbell clan stronghold in Scotland.

In 1908 Otekaieke was sold to the Crown for £97,000 and subdivided. Great changes took place: Robert Campbell's mansion became a residential school for backward or underprivileged boys, and was known as Campbell Park. When the school closed Campbell Park was taken over by the Waitaki County Council. Today it was privately owned and not open to the general public.

Dickson Jardine, the manager on Otekaieke at the time of its sale, was granted the homestead block and The Run, some of the country out back stretching away to Danseys Pass. Travelling between his two blocks meant crossing Kenmore, someone else's land, and that would always be a bone of contention on Otekaieke.

Dickson Jardine held Otekaieke until 1913, when William H. Munro, of the well-known Waitaki family, took it over. On Munro's death in 1922 the station came into the hands of his widow and her foster son, J. George McDonald. McDonald married and eventually the station was passed on to his two children Wendy and Robin. In 1960 Wendy's husband, Michael Bayley, purchased Robin's half of Otekaieke.

At the time of my visit, the Bayleys intended to winter 9000 Merino sheep and 800 cattle. I had seen some of their crossbred cattle out near Danseys Pass, grazing on a steep mountain-face. Those cattle had looked almighty small in such big country.

Tony Bayley has spent all of his working life on Dansey's old station.

Nowadays Mike Bayley, who was not from a farming background, was more than happy to let his son Tony handle things on the station. Tony had spent all of his working life on Otekaieke and was passionately interested in the land. All going to plan, he would own Otekaieke station one day.

Wendy and I strolled around the homestead gardens, which, despite the season and the gloomy day, looked especially good: lawns trimmed, flowerbeds weeded. It was a delightful setting with all the introduced trees framing it all and reminding me of England.

I knew that in Robert Campbell's time there would have been many gardeners on the staff, but when I asked Wendy if she had any help she gave her characteristic low, throaty laugh. "I'm it!" she said. "Times are tough."

FIVE

VALLEY OF THE AHURIRI

"Fancy mince on toast?" Ron Williamson said in the sunny kitchen of his home on Birchwood station. He nodded at a pan on the stove. "Plenty left." Ron's wife Jennifer was away for the day and Ron was obviously making out for himself.

I wasn't hungry, but it was good to know that back-country hospitality was alive and kicking up the Ahuriri.

"But you'll have a brew, won't you. Tea? Coffee?"

Now in his 57th year, Ron Williamson had known no other life but that of a high-country runholder, known no other place to call home but the magnificent Ahuriri valley. That was his good fortune. The other side of the coin showed in 1967 at the Timaru Show when, while competing in a horse event, Ron was crushed by his mount after a fall.

"It broke my back," he said matter-of-factly as he extracted a cigarillo from a slim packet and considered it. "But it's amazing what you can do if you set your mind to it, isn't it?" He lit his smoke and drew deeply on it. As he smiled through the curling smoke his eyes lit up too, a brilliant blue. You could warm to Ron Williamson real quick. "Can't complain, eh?"

An electric jug came to a boil and demanded Ron's attention. "Dad owned a small farm near Elephant Hill." Elephant Hill station was in the lower Waitaki valley. "He came out here to manage this place in the early forties."

To be precise, it was in 1942 that Ted Williamson

The Ahuriri valley.

58

and his wife came out to Birchwood. The station was then owned by Donald Grant and Jessie Lindley Lowry; they were among a good number of owners who had leased the station since the early 1870s. Ron would have been four years old when he moved there.

"What was it like growing up here?" I asked.

Ron's smile was a tad rueful. "Like?" He shook his head. "It wasn't easy. Mum had three small kids to look after. There was no water laid on – we had to carry that from the creek. No power or telephone, either. The road you came in on isn't the best even now but in those days it was no better than a bullock track. Sometimes it'd take you half a day to get out to the main road."

I digested that. As recently as 1942 Ron's family had lived very much the same way as the early settlers of the previous century. Not much more than fifty years ago – in my lifetime. Incredible!

Officially, Birchwood was transferred from D. Grant to E.M. Williamson in 1950, along with 4523 sheep, 570 cattle and 24 horses. Wool production had doubled since 1944–45, and the grazing area was listed at 12,500 hectares out of a total run of 24,000 hectares. Rabbits were regarded as few. From the homestead area the valley extended another 30 kilometres at least, and some of the station's country was in the Dingle Burn, which drained into Lake Hawea. The number of horses on Birchwood indicated they were top priority. While Ron's accident had ended his days of competitive riding, it didn't stop him mounting up for a full day on

Annabel and Simon Williamson outside their much altered Rabbit Board cottage.

the hill once a long period of convalescence was behind him.

"Of course," he was saying, "the really big change around here was when the power came on."

"What did your mother make of that?"

He shook his head. "Mum? No, she was gone by then." A flicker, no more, of sadness crossed his face. "Another big change was when we started growing our own hay. That was sixteen years ago." He added dryly, "Winters were pretty tough on the stock before then."

"What stock are you carrying?"

"Around 8000 sheep. We winter 450 cattle – some of the heifers are in the upper reaches of the Dingle Burn now." I hoped they enjoyed heaps of snow. "Simon pretty much looks after the cattle these days."

The Williamsons had two sons; Simon at 29 was the eldest. Henry, now in his mid-twenties, had been one of the mustering gang on Mount Nicholas station when I'd saddled up and gone along with them for the fall muster of 1990.

"What's Henry up to now?" I asked. Last I'd heard of him, he was still on Mount Nicholas.

"Henry? Oh, he's over in Western Australia, he's thinking of buying some land there – it's pretty cheap compared with here." Time for another cigarillo. "Course," he added with heavy emphasis, "he hasn't put in a summer there yet." He chuckled. "I expect he'll change his mind about that."

At that point Simon joined us. Wearing blue jeans and a woollen sweater over a wool shirt, he looked very much like both his father and his brother: they were all high-country people in every way. Lanky Simon smiled easily; he came across to me as a very relaxed, slow-talking type, slow to ruffle. But I knew it was a big mistake to underestimate that type of boy.

Simon took me over to the ex-Rabbit Board cottage he and his wife Annabel lived in. Formerly a Mackenzie, she came from Braemar station in, appropriately enough, the Mackenzie Country. The 25,500-hectare property had been in the Mackenzie family since the early 1960s.

Annabel indicated her dark-blue moleskins and fashionable creamy-coloured sweater. "I don't usually dress like this about the place," she laughed. "I'm just off to visit friends." And with that she departed.

Their home, Simon explained, had originally been located on Omarama station, one of a number of buildings owned by the now obsolete Rabbit Board. He thought they dated to the late 1950s or the early 1960s. The Williamsons bought it cheaply, then had it transported by road. Its new location was a grand setting, with the Barrier Range across the river and high snowy peaks whichever way you cared to look.

They had set to work to transform the dwelling: the end result was a delightful little home decorated in striking dark greens and bold blues, where a wood-burning stove heated the entire floor space. There were lots of knick-knacks scattered about – magazines, books, broad-brimmed hats, even the shoulder-mounted heads of thar and chamois.

"Annabel can take all the credit for it," Simon said, proud of what his wife of just 18 months had achieved.

"Tell her I'm impressed," I said and, even as I said the words, it occurred to me that most of the Rabbit Board boys I'd known would have thought they were in the wrong place here.

Outside Simon and I stood side by side and looked across the broad river flatlands to the rearing mass of land that was the Barrier Range – thar and chamois country.

"What about deer?" I asked.

" No, there aren't too many of those around now," Simon replied rather cagily.

Back in the aftermath of the Second World War, the Ahuriri country had been one of the prime deerculling blocks. Earlier Ron had rattled off some names I knew well: Jack McNair, who had published *Shooting for the Skipper* in 1971; Jim Ollerenshaw, a hunter turned field officer whose ability with a camera had eclipsed anything he'd ever done with a hot-barrelled .303; and the near-legendary Frank Woolf, who'd once shot over 2000 deer in an eight-month summer season. Even today there were still old Forestry (now DoC) huts and tent-camps scattered about the mid-to-upper valley. The Ahuriri valley was also a breeding ground for a

The Ahuriri River and the Barrier Range.

Jim Morris (right) and Hunter Harrison working with Merinos at Ben Avon.

number of birds, among them black swan, black stilt, paradise duck and Canada goose. On the way in I'd seen all species but black stilt.

So here it was that Simon and Henry, just like their father before them, had grown up. Later Henry, of course, drifted away, but Simon had been here for all of his life; as the elder son it was taken for granted. I doubted if that had ever troubled the likes of Simon Williamson.

Leaving Birchwood station, heading downvalley, I soon jolted over a cattle-grid gateway and found myself on Ben Avon. Located roughly midway up the Ahuriri valley, the station, as was a part of Birchwood, was once Longslip station. Taken up in 1858, Longslip had been over 40,000 hectares in size and extended over the mountains to Lake Hawea. Ben Avon, with its homestead, woolshed and so on, was an out-station to the main Longslip complex. As with Birchwood, Ben Avon's history was rather muddled. It appeared to have become totally separate from Longslip in 1906, when Hugh Edward Cameron took it on.

Today Ben Avon was owned by Jim Morris, and he and Hunter Harrison were working with sheep in the yards when I first spotted them. It was the kind of scene that summed up station country for me: the men, the sheep, the dogs working as though their one big feed a day depended upon it, the big old woolshed, and, as a backdrop, the magnificent snowy mountains under a blue sky. The men worked as we talked.

On Ben Avon they ran 7500 Merinos and wintered 250 cattle on 10,000 hectares, Jim informed me. The rugged 47-year-old had been here for eight years, and before that he had been up the Rakaia on Manuka Point station. Sadly, he had lost his wife a few years ago.

Meantime, Hunter Harrison was giving an unwilling hogget a dose of something good for it; that was the general idea, anyhow. He'd spent four years on Molesworth under long-serving manager Don Reid before coming here.

Jim told me the woolshed dated to the 1880s and, originally, it had 24 stands. I wondered how many Ahuriri winds it had withstood in all that time.

Correspondence School time for Kate Emmerson and Debra Morris.

The original homestead on Ben Avon, and even subsequent ones, had long gone. Jim Morris's house was comparatively new, more in keeping with suburbia than the rugged back-country. It was at the homestead that I caught up with Kate, the 25-year-old daughter of Russell and Jeanette Emmerson of Forest Range station, over the Lindis Pass from the Ahuriri. Kate had spent five years overseas before, at a loose end, taking up a position as cook, housekeeper and teacher for Jim's six-year-old daughter Debra.

Kate explained that the Correspondence School lessons were easy to follow, although you could, of course, vary them. Today Kate had read Debra a story; then Debra had read her a story. Then they had read a brand-new story about pigeons. They had talked about pigeons after reading it and made a paper pigeon. Debra had even written a story about a pigeon. Later she had practised her printing then listened to a music tape. Kate told me that sometimes they danced to the music. And after that had come maths – not Debra's favourite subject, which gave me one thing in common with this particular six-year-old.

"What's your favourite subject, Debra?"

Debra was too shy to reply.

"Poetry," Kate said. "Debra's very good at that."

Later that day I caught up with Kate and Debra again. School must have been over for the day because they were out riding. It was at mid-afternoon – warm, windless, a mellow sort of afternoon. Spring was thinking about coming back to the valley of the Ahuriri River.

"Not a bad life?" I said to Kate.

"No," she replied with a winning smile.

Ben Avon cattle ranging the valley bottom.

SIX

OVER THE HAKATARAMEA PASS

On Round Hill station, up the valley of the Hakataramea, Grant McCrae was telling me that the incredibly powerful westerly wind that was blowing this April day wasn't an everyday happening. Just as well: this was a wild, rampaging wind strong enough to rip roofs off woolsheds. Perhaps it wasn't quite that strong: the roof was still in place on the woolshed here. This particular shed had stood for a mighty long time, Grant told me. It was built on Whalesback station in the Mackenzie Country in 1867 and in 1884 had been dismantled and transported by bullock wagon over the Hakataramea Pass to its present site.

I indicated some of Grant McCrae's 2800 hectares with a broad sweep of a hand: "This must've been all Hakataramea station back then?"

He nodded his fine, bearded head. "Yeah, all Haka. My place was taken off it in 1925."

As I pressed on up the true right of the river, the range across the Hakataramea was The Hunters Hills. Once most of it was covered with near impenetrable thickets of speargrass. The Maori name of Hakataramea translated as "the dance of the speargrass" or, simply, "dancing speargrass". It was all to do with the way the speargrass shook to the not so merry tune of the wind. The early sheepmen needed to burn off the speargrass and, since fire did not differentiate, the magnificent grasslands had gone as well. There was always a price to pay.

The Hunters Hills contain the eastern side of the Hakataramea River.

Grant McCrae on Round Hill station.

At the Hakataramea Pass there was a closed gate and a sign, the worse for wear, which said the altitude was 915 metres. It was a high, wind-blasted spot, raw and yet beautiful. The wind was very cold; this was no place to linger. I went on, into the Mackenzie Country. There wasn't a sheep in sight.

The first European to come this way – in 1855 – was a 25-year-old Englishman, George Dunnage, on a horse he purchased in Christchurch for £75 (horses were as hard to come by in early Christchurch as they were in Dunedin). His intention was to identify good grazing land in the unknown region where the sheep-stealer, James Mackenzie, had been apprehended a few months earlier.

"There was," he would write, "a small accommodation house at the Rakaia, and a guide to point out the ford." Dunnage crossed the Rakaia, and then the Rangitata, without difficulty but, although his horse behaved admirably, he wrote, "I did not like the large boulders." He worked his way steadily towards Burke Pass and found the country "pretty level and good for riding".

The only living creature I came across was an occasional wild pig, which scampered away at my approach.

At length I came to a low saddle leading into the Mackenzie plains. I camped for the night at the foot of the spur. Next morning I saddled up and resumed my journey. The plains were very rough riding, not only stony, but bestrewed with large boulders and sharp spaniards [speargrass], of which my horse did not approve.

I came to Lake Tekapo, and followed down the river bearing that name for some distance. I then made for a low saddle, now known as Whale's Back, and came to the Hakataramea Pass, then

The Mackenzie monument.

and his brothers would remain on Three Springs until the mid-1860s.

There appeared to be no name for the rough unsealed route I travelled. Suffice to say it linked Kurow on the Waitaki with Burke Pass in the Mackenzie Country, in a direct line about 80 kilometres apart. There was a time when Hakataramea station extended for pretty much all of this distance. Indeed, shepherds working on the place, if asked to define the station's southern and northern boundaries, were likely to say, "from the back of the Hakataramea Pub to the back of the Burke Pass Pub". Certainly it was a damn long way between cold beers on a stinking hot day.

At its peak, back when the New Zealand & Australian Land Co. Ltd ran things, Hakataramea was

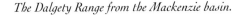

The Dalgety Range from the Mackenzie basin.

unknown, which led to the Waitaki River. From here I took an easterly direction and found Mackenzie's Pass, which was both difficult and dangerous to tackle with a horse. I managed, however, to get through safely, and I was now on my road back to Christchurch, which I reached after ten days' exciting experience.

Dunnage was keen on the Mackenzie Country and made two more trips before deciding against taking up a run within the huge basin itself. Instead, he secured the 6000-hectare Run 233, close to Fairlie. This was good, easy country near the Opihi River. There were three springs of fresh running water, sweet to the taste, so Three Springs station it became. George Dunnage

79,000 hectares in size and carried around 80,000 sheep. Part of this huge run was Whalesback station, which in 1873 had become part of Hakataramea and was in effect its northern boundary.

A lone harrier hawk, near motionless yet quivering, hovered perhaps 10 metres above the tall grasses on the lower slopes of the Grampian Mountains. Suddenly the hawk folded its winds and dropped as though it was a heavy stone. What had it taken? A rabbit? A field mouse?

The Grampian Mountains were named after the highest range in Scotland, where Ben Nevis stood tallest of all. The mountains gave the name to a 24,000-hectare run taken on by Harry Ford in 1858. Two of the early shepherds on The Grampians were George and John McCrae. They often put in a stint of boundary keeping at a sod hut somewhere below the pass I'd just come down from. By all accounts, John wore a kilt as his regular working garb. Hardy John would've known all about those strong winds, all right.

Rampaging winds, heavy snows and baking hot summers were part and parcel of life on the high Mackenzie plain. You needed the bark on, as well as a thick woollen kilt, to make it out there. Basically you needed to be a Highland shepherd to see it through: by the mid-1880s, almost all of the early English runholders, coming from a far kinder climate and a considerably more genteel way of life than their Scottish counterparts, had either packed it in and gone home or taken on a property closer to civilisation.

Most of the raw-boned Scots in the Mackenzie Country conversed in Gaelic; the kilt was worn at most social functions, rather like a badge of pride. They were men of strong principles not known for humour. When they travelled beyond Burke Pass they talked of going

Dusk on a winter's evening at Lake Tekapo.

The Church of the Good Shepherd.

"down country". This was not only a geographical description: it also had strong moral implications.

At a junction in the road, I paused to let a four-wheel-drive ute rattle by. The driver wore a big hat and a huntaway stood on the back of the ute with his big paws on the roof of the cabin. The driver waved a hand out the window. He had come from the south, towards the Waitaki. That way led to a number of stations: The Grampians, Streamlands, Grays Hill, Haldon and Black Forest. All up there were about 42 high-country runs out there in the Mackenzie catchment.

I followed the ute north and soon came to the Snow River. The "Snowy", which came down from the Dalgety Range, was running low, a creek really. A few rabbits were on show, a few seagulls, but no stock. There wasn't much for sheep or cattle to feed on where the Snow River crossed the plains country.

In 1911 Mount Dalgety station came into being when 13,000 hectares of Hakataramea station (the old Whalesback run) was taken over by the Government and split into two properties. Chilton Hayter named his station after Mount Dalgety (1752 metres) at the far, southern end of his property, while William Quirke saw no good reason why the name Whalesback should not be reinstated for his western section.

With a growing sense of anticipation I pressed on towards the Mackenzie Pass. Once across the small Mackenzie River, I found what I was looking for on a grassy verge. In a lovely spot with the sun streaming down, the pipits and skylarks singing away and the wind elsewhere, was a monument, a three-cornered cairn with an inscription carved in English, Gaelic and Maori. In English it read: "In this spot James Mackenzie the freebooter was captured by John Sidebottom and the Maoris Taiko and 'Seventeen' and escaped from them the same night. 4th March 1855."

The story of what happened next to James

Mackenzie had been told many times but, sheep stealer that he was, Mackenzie was also an explorer who discovered new country. The pass named after him, and through which he took his stolen sheep, more-or-less separated the Dalgety Range from the Rollesby Range.

Other station mailboxes flashed by as I went on to Burke Pass. The last time I had travelled this road, in winter 1992, these stations were under deep snow and right out of feed. They battled through – somehow station people always did.

Perhaps it was the sense of enormous spaciousness about the Mackenzie Country that really appealed to me, that feeling of not being contained. Perhaps many of the early runholders felt much the same way when they put Burke Pass behind them and, suddenly, the great, high plain opened up before them, stretching towards what they called the Snowy Mountains and the unknown country beyond.

The bronze sheep dog.

To the west of Burke Pass, on the shores of the grand high-country lake of Tekapo, stood the Church of the Good Shepherd. It was built of local stone in 1935 as a memorial to the pioneer settlers of the Mackenzie Country. The church faced out over the lake, looking towards station country; the Good Shepherd kept an eye on those steep mountainfaces, the strong men and the near tireless dogs that scrambled up the steep slopes, the Merinos that rushed before them.

A good shepherd, of course, was nothing without the services of a good dog. Any shepherd worth hiring knew full well the true value of a sheepdog and it was something you really could not put a price on. So it was wonderful that the part the sheepdog played in the Mackenzie Country had been recognised: near the Church of the Good Shepherd stood a bronze sheepdog. He was positioned on a stone cairn, a collie, ears pricked, ready to respond in a finger-snap of time to whatever his beloved master asked of him. Behind the dog rose the Two Thumb Range, near the stone cairn was a clump of matagouri.

This bronze sheepdog was the work of Innes Elliot, wife of a local runholder. Many regarded it as a monument to James Mackenzie's dog Friday, but the real intention was that it be representative of all the untold dogs that had lived out their lives in the Mackenzie Country.

There was a brass plaque embedded in the stone cairn.

This monument was erected by the runholders of the Mackenzie Country and those who appreciate the value of the collie dog, without the help of which the grazing of this mountain country would be impossible. Unveiled on March 7, 1968 by Sir Arthur Porritt, Bt, GCMM, KCVO, CBE, Governor General of New Zealand.

Beannahden air cu caoragh.

The heartfelt words written in Gaelic might have been said in gratitude by many a good Scottish shepherd, here in the Mackenzie Country or back home in the Highlands: "Blessings on the dog".

Overleaf: Romneys on Glenburn Station, Wairarapa.

NORTHERN
LANDS

Ihungia
Ruangatehu • Pukeiti

Tangihau

Kakariki •
Kaiwaka • Okepuha
Ngamatea • Timahanga Onenui
Ohinewairua • Maraekakaho

Otairi •

Flat Point Caledonia
Arawhata
Waimoana
Wharekaka Glenburn

SEVEN

THE ROMNEY FACTOR

On a rather murky Good Friday, Tony Pearce was single-handedly drenching sheep in the muddy yards. The place was Ngakaraka, out of Masterton, beyond the scattered settlement of Te Wharau on a winding back-country road that would eventually take me to the coast and, at road's end, Glenburn station. In the Te Wharau district there were at least 40 properties, ranging from small, farm-sized places like Tony's to genuine stations – the coastal runs of Caledonia, Flat Point and, biggest of all, Glenburn.

I complimented Tony on his good-looking Romneys and he, being a sheepman, was well pleased. "Two-tooths?" I went on, an educated guess.

Tony bobbed his head up and down in confirmation.

(When a sheep is weaned, at about eight months, it becomes known as a hogget rather than a lamb. In this period it grows two milk teeth, which are replaced with two permanent teeth at around 16 or 18 months; at this stage they are no longer hoggets and the term "two-tooths" applies. From then on they grow two more teeth each year and become, in turn, four-tooths and six-tooths, until, of course, they have a full mouth.)

Tony Pearce raised an eyebrow at me. "Going to Glenburn, you say? Top place. Best on the coast. You picked a good time to visit – the dog trials are on tomorrow."

"I know. You going?"

Tony Pearce working with his young Romneys.

"Yeah. Wouldn't miss it for quids. Real big event around here. You met Gwyn yet?" Gwyn Williamson was the manager on Glenburn.

"Only talked with him on the phone."

Tony gestured at the sheep with the muzzle of his drenching gun. "Better get on with it, eh?"

"What's the weather going to do?"

He looked briefly to the overcast sky. He shook his head; there were no real answers up there. "Be a bastard if it rains tomorrow."

And so I left him to it: Tony Pearce, back bent, working his Romney two-tooths on his own. On a public holiday, too.

I pressed on towards the coast through a vividly green landscape dotted with sheep. It occurred to me that, just about anywhere you cared to travel in this country, you could see sheep.

I'd done my research on the subject of sheep: in ballpark figures there was a base flock of around 50 million sheep in New Zealand, which meant that sheep outnumbered people by well over 12 to one in a landmass about the size of Britain. New Zealand was undoubtedly a land of sheep.

Although New Zealand was well down the world list in terms of numbers of sheep, it was the world's largest producer of crossbred wool – that is, strong wool – contributing 25 percent of the world's overall total. This

The Romney statue at Gore.

type of wool was used mainly in interior textiles: carpets, upholstery, furnishing, rugs, bedding, hand-knitting yarns and blankets. The country was also, I discovered, the world's largest exporter of sheep meat: each year we exported around 27 million lambs and 7 million sheep for food consumption.

The most common breed of sheep was the Romney – it accounted for about 46 percent of the national flock – and a long way back in second place was the Coopworth, followed by the Perendale. The Coopworth and Perendale were, in fact, both the result of careful cross breeding of Romney with other breeds, so the vital Romney factor was evident in about 66 percent of the national flock. The Romney was found in all the sheep-raising regions, with the exception of the light rainfall areas of Otago, Canterbury and Marlborough, which were Merino range.

The New Zealand Romney story started with an English breed of sheep that didn't mind getting its feet wet on the lush pasturelands of southern Kent. The Romney Marsh was first introduced into New Zealand in 1853 when four rams and 16 ewes were landed at Wellington by Leonard Young, who sold them on to a Hutt Valley farmer called Alfred Ludlam.

The first Romney stud in New Zealand, at Waiorongomai station, was started by Alfred Matthews in 1875 when he purchased 83 ewes and lambs bred by Ludlam. By the turn of the century there were at least 100 Romney stud flocks in New Zealand and the

A Perendale ewe feeding her lamb on the banks of the Matukituki River, Mount Aspiring station, Otago.

popularity of the breed, particularly in the wetter regions of the North Island, was second to none.

Over a period of time in New Zealand, the Romney Marsh altered its physiology enough to be recognised as a separate breed: the New Zealand Romney. It was bigger than its ancestors, was leaner, and had longer legs, the better to climb with.

The Coopworth sheep was named after Professor Ian Coop, who in the late 1950s and early 1960s was in charge of its early development. The breed, the result of a Romney/Border Leicester cross, was an easy-care sheep with excellent mothering abilities and stress-free lambing, meaning there was far less work for a shepherd to do. The Coopworth, used for both wool and meat, would become a remarkable success story in New Zealand and eventually it would be exported to Eastern Europe, the United States and, most of all, Australia.

The Perendale, however, preceded the Coopworth as New Zealand's first "home-grown" easy-care sheep. The tale dated as far back as 1928 and its main player was Geoffrey Peren, one of the founders of Massey Agricultural College (later Massey University). At that time the Romney was of course the most popular breed of sheep in the North Island, although the Romney/ Lincoln cross was not uncommon.

All things considered, most Romney raisers on hill-country properties were dissatisfied with the breed. The Romney, they said, was not hardy enough and its fertility rate left much to be desired. What was required was a crossbred sheep that would retain the time-tested qualities of the Romney and improve on them. Finding the solution to the problem would become a labour of love for Geoffrey Peren, the English-born but Canadian-raised Professor of Agriculture. During the 1940s he mated the finest examples of hardy Cheviot rams with Romney ewes, and the very best of their offspring were chosen to form the foundations of the breed that would carry the professor's name: the Perendale.

The Perendale that was finally turned out onto hard North Island country in 1961 was a small-to-medium animal with sturdy legs bare of wool. The Cheviot input was most noticeable in the pricked, alert ears and the keen eyes, and especially about the long aristocratic face with its Roman nose. On the hill, the Perendale proved tough and largely self-sufficient, lambing successfully without shepherding. It was less susceptible to internal parasites than other breeds.

When mustered, the flighty Perendale responded quickly: it could be driven home to station headquarters in double-quick time. Left to its own devices, however, it moved freely about its range, always curious about what was over the next hill. Lamb production was up over the Romney by 10–15 percent.

The introduction of the Cheviot genes did not, however, enhance the woolclip – at an average of 3.5 kilograms, the Perendale's fleece was a kilogram lighter than that of a Romney. On the credit side, Perendale wool was finer in quality, more resilient, bulkier and whiter in colour.

The Romney also played a key role in the development of the Drysdale sheep, whose wool was used exclusively for carpet manufacture. Back in 1931 Dr Francis Dry, an English-born geneticist at Massey Agricultural College, came across a genetic freak while working with Romney sheep – a heavy-horned ram with extremely coarse fibre running through its fleece. Dry mated this ram with Romney and Cheviot ewes of a similar wool type to produce an animal that grew long, coarse wool that had to be shorn twice a year. Today there were some 350 Drysdale sheep raisers in the country and the flock stood at around 550,000.

Unexpectedly the heavy cloud barrier, with its

The woolshed on Arawhata station.

With thunder blasting about the Victoria Range in Westland, Drysdale ewes tend to their young.

promise of rain, broke up and brilliant late-afternoon sunshine greeted my arrival on the low green hills overlooking the sea. On a day such as this – the sun shining, the light breeze warm, the air so good to breathe – there would be few places in the country to match the Wairarapa coastline.

I drove slowly as the road wound down the hill past possum-mutilated cabbage trees in shallow gullies. Sheep scattered every which way. Presently I came to a hairpin bend, where I stopped and looked down to coastal flats at the southern end of what had once been Flat Point station.

The station was first taken up by C.F. Hales and Phillip Murch in the 1850s, making it one of the oldest Wairarapa runs. The Cameron family came on the scene in 1908 when Charlie acquired Flat Point, which then took in about 10,000 hectares. He died in 1943, leaving the station to his three sons, who divided it up in 1956. The eldest son, Crawford, retained the gracious homestead given to him and his bride as a wedding present by his father in 1929 – at the southern end of the run. Crawford called his 2000-hectare station Waimoana. Brother Eric took over the main, central homestead and kept the name Flat Point for his run, while brother Geoffrey ended up with what had been the northern end of Flat Point, and this he called Caledonia.

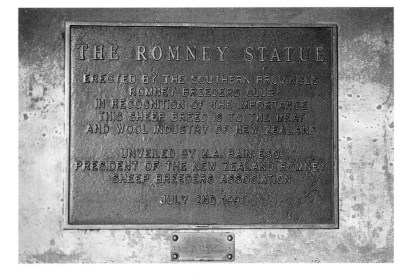

In 1977 Crawford, getting on in years, retired to Masterton and his two sons split up Waimoana evenly between them and another new station, called Arawhata, was born. Today John and Mary McGuines were on Flat Point station and Hamish and Kerry Goodwin could be found on Caledonia. The Camerons retained Arawhata and the picturesque woolshed I could now see from my vantage point.

I hit the road and soon came to Glenburn's signposted boundary. Ahead was a lovely sight: the dazzling blue of the sea with seabirds wheeling above the pounding surf, then the narrow coastal flats and their stands of karaka trees, leaves of emerald green, and the hills beyond, hemming in the flats, rising sharply and dotted with sheep and cattle.

I hadn't noticed a rather battered four-wheel-drive vehicle jolting behind me. I pulled to the side of the road to let it pass. The driver tooted his horn and waved a hand. I replied with the thumbs-up sign, wondering if it was someone heading to Glenburn for the dog trials.

In no hurry at all, I killed the engine and poured myself a cup of lukewarm coffee from a flask. As I sipped it in the sun I gazed at a paddock full of greybacks – several thousand at least, and all Romneys.

EIGHT

SIMPLY GLENBURN

The ever-cheerful Connie Tehuki put a more than generous helping of crispy bacon and plump mushrooms before me in the well-appointed cookshop on Glenburn station.

"Hope you like mushrooms?" Connie the cook was pencil-slim, thirtyish and not unattractive.

"Love mushrooms," I told her, buttering a piece of toast.

"Good. We pick them ourselves."

"Even better."

"Plenty more if you want them."

I smiled: toast and coffee were my usual breakfast fodder. "Hey, I'm not a 20-year-old shepherd, you know."

I ate a solitary breakfast while Connie rattled pans next door. Local legend King Riddiford, who'd once owned Glenburn as well two of the other coastal Wairarapa stations I'd visited – Te Awaiti and Orongorongo – couldn't have been better looked after.

I had been up before daybreak, well in advance of the local sparrows, on a cool rather than cold day. While it was still dark I had driven along the coast and about midway between the Glenburn and Waimoana homesteads I'd watched the sun rise out of a dead calm sea and I'd marvelled at it in the way that a pagan might have.

Little matey bunches of Romneys, scattered along the foreshore, had watched with me the ascent of the

Above: Connie Tehuki, right: Another day begins on Glenburn.

sun, the bringer of warmth and light. What did they make of it all? I knew they ran about 12,000 breeding ewes on Glenburn's 6000 hectares and that they had a special Romney breeding programme. Naturally enough, the Romneys, to a sheep, had turned to watch me. They'd looked contented enough. Romney range didn't get any better than the frost-free, sun-drenched Wairarapa coastline.

By the time I'd returned to station headquarters all of the men had had their breakfast, but Connie had told me to turn up for a feed no matter what time it was. I'd always been good at turning up for a feed.

"More coffee?" Connie the cook was back again, hovering at my shoulder like a mother hen.

"Terrific!"

"Seen the porpoises out there?" She nodded towards a window that overlooked the sea. In the distance a school of porpoises sliced effortlessly through the white-flecked swell. It was a fantastic sight and, I expect, one unique to Glenburn. "Often see them out there."

I slowly sipped my coffee and contemplated the sea.

Back in the old days all of the station's woolclip had been taken out by steamer. The vessels anchored well offshore, 300 metres away at least, and the wool was transferred and station supplies off-loaded in big surfboats. They used bullock-drawn drays and, later, wagons, to transport the bales of wool from the shed to the surfboat. Bullocks were ideal, slow but rock-steady

Connie's daughter Lisa and her pet Romney lamb.

in a crisis. Patiently they would stand belly-deep in the sea while the bales were manhandled from wagon to surfboat.

Often schools of curious porpoises came in close to the shore just to see what was going on in their territory. Sometimes they would swim very close to the bullocks, and might even brush playfully against a bullock's leg. No matter: a bullock was too much of a stoic to let that type of thing upset it. By the early 1920s the bullocks had been replaced by a four-strong team of horses. The horses were terrified of the gregarious porpoises, sleek demons of the sea. Crawford Cameron, up the coast a bit, found an effective way of keeping the over-friendly porpoises at a good distance: he cracked his stock whip at them repeatedly. The dolphin-like porpoises were intelligent enough to know when they were not wanted.

Breakfast over, I carried my dirty dishes into the kitchen. Connie sat at a table with two of her friends, a Maori woman and a Pakeha man. Smoko appeared to consist of something much stronger than Bell tea and too many smokes. Still, it was a holiday weekend.

Outside, I stretched on the cookshop veranda. It was wonderfully warm. It was difficult to really believe it was fall muster time on the big South Island runs. Nearby a crowd of people were talking and laughing. Most of them were staying for the long weekend, camped in the station's motel-like accommodation.

Glenburn's Gwyn and Lindy Williamson and their four daughters, home from school, were also entertaining friends. Moreover, vehicles were arriving from other parts of the Wairarapa as competitors in the dog trials put in an appearance.

There were kids all over the show. One of Gwyn and Lindy's daughters – Nikky, it looked like – trotted happily by on her pony with a couple of her friends riding alongside her. Connie's daughter Lisa was playing with her friends. A fat little lamb trailed after

and his brother Ken's place, Otairi station. Indeed I had! I recalled it used to be a big place, and Doug confirmed it was.

"Been in the same family well over a hundred years now," he went on. He seemed very proud of that fact.

"Not many stations you can say that about today," I pointed out.

He gave me a thoughtful look. "Listen, why don't you call in at Otairi on your way back home? It's nothing out of your way." He paused. "Give me a call

Alan Schnell.

Bruce Harding.

Hamish Cavanagh.

her, and Larry the Romney didn't look none too bright upstairs.

On this Easter Saturday Glenburn station was starting to resemble a three-ring circus minus the clowns.

One of the people staying here was a slim, dark type of middle years and average height wearing snug-fitting moleskins much cleaner than mine. He paused for a chat and it turned out he was one Douglas Duncan from Hunterville way. He asked me if I had heard of his

a day or two before you come, okay?"

Sometimes it all fell into place as neatly and as easily as that.

Around mid-morning the Glenburn sheepdog trials got underway, the various events taking place simultaneously on the low hills not far from the 89-year-old homestead. On these top-dressed slopes facing the sea rowdy huntaways and silent heading dogs were going to make their master's day or they weren't. Either way, they'd have quite a time of it.

Sheepdog trials in New Zealand were said to have started on Hakataramea station in South Canterbury in 1889, 13 years after the first recorded sheepdog trials were held in Wales. The North Island Sheepdog Trials Association dated to 1910 and its South Island equivalent to 1932. The first national sheepdog trials took place at Hawera in 1936. It would be 1956 before the North and South Island associations merged to become the New Zealand Sheepdog Trials Association.

Among those watching the Glenburn sheepdog trials was manager Gwyn Williamson. In his early forties, he was blond, well built, good-looking, and taller than tall. Originally he came from Waituna West in the Manawatu, where his family still bred stud cows.

Earlier I'd asked him if he had any regrets about coming to the Wairarapa. "Absolutely not," he'd replied. "It's the most amazing environment for kids you could ever hope to find. Anyone with a sense of adventure can have a great time here. It's got everything: swimming, diving, great fishing, deer hunting in the hills and horse riding."

"Station life isn't too bad either, I suppose?"

The man had laughed before telling me what station folk had known for years in these parts: Glenburn was, and had always been, a top place to work on.

"Wouldn't have minded a job here when I was a young bloke," I'd said to Gwyn.

The classic New Zealand huntaway.

"Neither would I!" Gwyn had fired back.

Now as I hunkered down alongside Gwyn he smiled his easy smile.

"How're the boys doing?" I asked

Gwyn fingered his clean-shaven jaw. The boss might be taking life very easy today but there were standards to be kept up. "Pretty good, I think."

The "boys" were the regular shepherding team: Brian Pierce, Hamish Cavanagh, Alan Schnell and Bruce Harding. They were all taking an active part in the dog trials, and that meant a lot to Gwyn. It would mean considerably more to him if they did well.

I stretched out like Gwyn, my back to a fencepost, the sun on my face. "I hear Hamish is the man to beat."

Gwyn nodded his head at that. "Expect he is."

The young, smooth-faced Cavanagh, tanned and bursting with good health, came from his parents' Hawkdun station near St Bathans in Central Otago, Manuherikia River country. As likely as not the Shennan brothers had ridden over their land all those years ago, back when the tall tussocks stood belly high to a big horse.

Naturally enough, they ran Merinos on Hawkdun station. To my surprise they also ran Merinos on Glenburn – 3000 of them. Young Hamish Cavanagh was in charge of the Merino breeding programme and, of course, he was picking up a lot of pointers about

Romneys too. When Gwyn had mentioned Merinos to me, my ears had shot up like a startled Perendale's. How were they making out here? Great, was the answer. Indeed, it was Gwyn's intention to increase the Merino flock to 5000 over three years.

Meantime, in the dog trials, a competitor was putting his huntaway through its paces. The huntaway was putting the hard word on the bleating Romneys, who would have much preferred to have been somewhere else.

There were two competition classes for huntaways: the straight hunt and the zig-zag hunt. In both events sheep were set loose at the foot of the hills. The shepherd stayed there. The sheep were driven by his dog, which responded to his commands, working, barking, through a set of flags placed at regular intervals. The entire course was around 400 metres as a rule. The zig-zag variation meant just that.

It was a great dog, this huntaway – and a fully home-grown breed of dog, too, as Kiwi as New Zealand's first home-grown sheep, the Corriedale.

The working dogs the first Scottish shepherds brought to this country were heading dogs, which worked silently. The dogs were ideal in the misty Scottish highlands, where a keen-eyed shepherd could usually see one boundary fence from another, but in the high country of the South Island your everyday Border collie was as useful as teats on a bull. On the huge southern runs the sheep were spread far and wide, and they were often difficult to reach and almost impossible to shift.

What the shepherds needed was a dog that would tackle tough terrain without fuss and bark very loudly upon finding the sheep. They mated their very best barkers and bred selectively until they achieved a big, powerful, rangy dog that could run like the wind, was intelligent and seemingly tireless, and whose deep-toned barking carried for miles around the big tussocky basins. Took a power of beating, did a top huntaway.

Next in line in the huntaway trials was Alan Schnell,

The Glenburn station complex: stables at the extreme right, the long woolshed, and the homestead is behind the trees at the extreme left.

who, it turned out, had been a cadet at Smedley station at the time of my visit years earlier. Since then, he had worked on Otupae station on the high Inland Patea country. Alan wore an Akubra hat; appropriately enough, it was the Cattleman model – here on Glenburn he was, among other things, responsible for the welfare of the 1300 breeding cows.

By mid-afternoon the dog trials were already starting to wind down, and I drove up the winding four-wheel-drive access road behind the station complex. The track went clear over the main hump-backed coastal ridge to Glenburn's big hinterland. There was a lot of heavy bush country out there, Alan Schnell had told me, with deer, pigs and even wild cattle. Gwyn had explained that the cattle were Hereford crosses and they had been running wild for about 20 years. He'd also pointed out that they were potentially dangerous.

Midway to the crest of the ridge I stopped on a bench to look back at the nerve-centre of the station. Most of the green-painted buildings dated to about the same period that the Riddifords had built the homestead in 1907, and I'd found the stables especially interesting. The cookhouse, complete with accommodation, was a recent replacement for an old cookhouse that had burnt down.

Movement near the beachfront caught my attention: a bunch of riders jogging across the flats beyond the stables. The entire Williamson family had been riding on the beach, a fine way to spend part of an Easter Saturday afternoon.

Ian Cameron, the last Cameron on the coast in 1996.

I'd caught up with them a little earlier. They had made a great sight as they rode across the sandy beach towards me, pounding along at a near gallop, a miniature Welsh pony and a footsore dog bringing up the rear. The excited horses came to a lunging halt and milled about me, waiting for little Taffy to catch up.

Lanky Gwyn looked just fine on his big, powerfully built gelding Donk. Donk? No donkey this: the animal was tailor-made for the territory and it would need a big lump of horse to cart the likes of Gwyn around the steep Wairarapa hill country.

Gwyn told me he'd always liked horses: as a boy at Waituna West he had ridden to school on a pony. When he'd taken on the manager's job at Glenburn, he'd found the station horses were pretty much unused. That was hard to understand – this was ideal horse country. A man could see much more of the country from the back of a horse, so he could control his dogs better; and the lack of a trailbike's jarring noise was almost certainly kinder on the stock. A man on horseback was more in harmony with the environment than a man on a trailbike. As Gwyn put it, it was a "damn nice way to work".

When I returned to the station complex there was movement afoot. In the big, sprawling woolshed, they were having a social get-together: a barbecue, music, a little dancing, perhaps, and the prize-giving for the trials. The beer was flowing and the party had begun. The men were mostly grouped together and the women likewise, which said a great deal for communication between the sexes and none of it good. Rock music blared out and Connie the cook was one of the first to hit the dance floor.

For a time I chatted with Lynne Thompson of Waimoana, who told me she loved it up here. They were doing farmstays on Waimoana, she added, and this holiday weekend a Wellington couple were staying with them. Waimoana was less than three hours from their place to Wellington, but it might as well be light years away.

Ian Cameron from Arawhata station was there. He explained that Arawhata was up for sale. It wouldn't be long before he'd be gone; they were already calling him "the last Cameron on the coast". A pity, but there it was. It was the same old story: the famous Riddifords had gone from this part of the world too.

Today Glenburn was owned by two Wellington businessmen, Tim and Geoff Vogel, who had their own home on the place. It seemed to me that they couldn't have had a better man than the tall one running things for them.

As for Gwyn Williamson, well, he was nursing a beer and seemed to have a fixed grin on his face. Why not? His boys had done him, and the station, proud today. Hamish Cavanagh had dominated the events and Alan and Brian had won a prize or two as well. It was close to a clean sweep for the Glenburn boys at the dog trials of 1996.

The music was still pounding when I left the woolshed, Connie was still going strong, and the beer was far from out. There would be a few sore heads in the morning.

The Williamson family know how to enjoy themselves.

NINE

ON THE MAHIA PENINSULA

It was mid-morning at Onenui. Smoko. Around the table in the modern homestead sat station manager Brian Lloyd and two casual hands that might just as well have been family – Butch Pardoe and John Hawkins. If you mentioned any of those three names just about anywhere in the East Coast's station country they'd know who you were talking about. The Lloyds had been on the Peninsula for 13 good years. Before that Lloyd had been the manager on Waiomatatini, near Ruatoria.

The men were dressed in stockmen's clothing and they smelled of horse sweat. Earlier I had watched them bring cattle up from a coastal paddock to the stockyards. Riding horses was second nature to them, an accepted way of life. The station had its own herd of

brood mares and fine stallions, and there was no better horse breaker in these parts than Butch Pardoe.

After morning tea they planned to treat the yarded cattle for internal parasites using an external worm drench.

"More coffee?" Sally Lloyd asked me. The boss's wife had a nice easy way about her and a dignity that seemed to me inherent in the East Coast Maoris.

"Please." I slid my empty cup across the table to her.

You could come across stations in the most unexpected and unlikely locations. The Mahia Peninsula was one of those out-of-the-way places, a triangular landmass, quite hilly, that thrust southwards

Out at Jimmy's, on Timahanga station.

into the sea from the north-eastern extremity of Hawke Bay. It was 21 kilometres long, about 12 kilometres broad at its widest point, and its highest point, at 366 metres, was Te Kapu. The Maoris had a long association with Te Mahia, which means "indistinct sound" – a reference, perhaps, to the ripple of the streams, or to the sound of distant birds, or to the faraway roar of the breaking surf on Mahia Beach.

Onenui station, owned by over 1000 Maori shareholders, was the largest on the Mahia Peninsula, and its 3600 hectares covered more than half of the land. Much of the station was hilly, with steep ridges running down to 34 kilometres of coastline. There were some areas of native bush, which were home to wild cattle and feral pigs. They had 9000 breeding Romney/Perendale ewes and 600 crossbred cattle, as well as a few domestic pigs for home consumption – those I saw were foraging on a big pile of squash.

Despite the overcast conditions, the station country of the Mahia Peninsula was looking in tip-top condition, the grass Waikato green. Yet it was only a year earlier to the month that the entire Peninsula had been in the grip of an unrelenting drought and manager Brian Lloyd had taken to the road with 600 head of cattle in search of grazing. Sally had walked at the head of the cattle as they ambled along and Brian rode his white mount Cloud at the rear. Often they were given a hand by the likes of Butch Pardoe and John Hawkins and his wife, Leana. It was something like a holiday, Sally told me, and along the way they stayed with family and friends. They were away from the station for nearly five months but it was still pretty dry when they got back.

Portland Island, 1.2 kilometres offshore, was also under the control of Onenui station. The 141-hectare

The men working cattle on Onenui.

92

limestone tableland was well watered with natural springs and the station ran about 800 sheep there year-round. Shearing was done on the island each spring by Butch Pardoe's shearing gang: two top shearers, two shed hands who doubled as shearers and a couple of press-men.

The men saw shearing on Portland Island as a paid holiday. They were transported to the island by the station's aluminium crayfishing boat skippered by Tai Campbell (they harvested about 3 tonnes of crayfish), a trip that took about 20 minutes in good weather. Shearing of the ewes and lambs took two days, weather permitting. In their spare time – there was always time to spare on Portland Island when Butch Pardoe was boss – the gang donned wetsuits and dived and snorkelled along the shoreline. What a life!

Butch Pardoe liked to tell the story of a shearer who'd applied for a job with him. Just about the first thing that Butch Pardoe asked was, "You got a passport?"

"Eh?"

"You'll need one because you're going overseas."

"Overseas?"

"Yeah, you're going to Portland Island."

The shearer had caught on then.

"You can eat all the crays you want to there," Butch went on.

"I can eat crays by the sackful!" the shearer enthused.

True to his word, the shearer ate copious amounts of the delicacy – four crays for breakfast, two crays at smoko, one cray for lunch and six crays at tea-time.

On his second full day on Portland Island, the shearer tapped Butch on the shoulder: "When we gonna kill a mutton, boss?"

Early morning on the Mahia Peninsula.

The Portland Island woolclip, around 46 bales, was either flown out by helicopter or taken on the crayfishing boat. The boat was used to transport the shorn lambs to the mainland, up to 40 at a time. The distressed mothers were left behind like castaways. Who'd be a ewe at such a time?

Smoko: Butch Pardoe looked across the table at me. There was a whole lot of quiet dignity about him, too. "Where next?" he asked.

I hastily swallowed a piece of Maori bread. It was more cake like than anything else – good, too. "Ihungia," I finally said.

Butch Pardoe nodded his wise-looking head. "The horse sale, eh?"

"Uh-huh."

"Not good for the Coast," was his succinct comment.

"You're right there, Butch," Brian Lloyd said.

And John Hawkins grunted his agreement.

Butch was referring to the fact that Ihungia, the very essence of the East Coast station, would soon cease to exist. More than a century of stirring history didn't count for anything: Ihungia might just as well have been washed out to sea at Waipiro Bay on a tide forever outgoing.

"Let's get them cattle done," Brian Lloyd said. The men stood up as one. Another smoko on Onenui was over.

John Hawkins.

Butch Pardoe.

Where the hill country of the Mahia Peninsula suddenly fell away to form tablelands I found Okepuha station, the 1100-hectare property owned by Will Coop. Will was away on business when I called in to see Phil Turner, the 33-year-old stock manager and his wife Gabriella, a shepherd. Together they accounted for about 95 percent of all stock work.

Phil explained he worked first as a musterer on Jack Roberts's Timahanga station in the Inland Patea country. On the 12,500-hectare run, lying mostly south of the Napier-Taihape road, Jack ran Corriedales and Phil found them a dream to work with. When he talked with nostalgia of places like Jimmy's (an outlying house where one of Jack's sons lived) and the even more remote Pohokura out-station, I knew where he was coming from. I had first seen this great country when I was hunting for the Forest Service in the 1960s and just a year earlier I'd returned to it.

"See any deer?" Phil asked with a hunter's natural interest.

Sure, I'd seen deer – why, I'd even seen deer out in the open. Spotting me, they'd trotted off to a clump of isolated bush as though it didn't matter one way or another. Jack Roberts had always regarded Timahanga's backblocks as something of a game reserve: the only things missing were the NO HUNTING signs. It was like that now on a great many stations that were hard hit during the days of rampant helicopter hunting. Phil Turner had gone on to work as head shepherd on Hugh Lilburn's 2400-hectare Ferndale station, in the Hunterville district, and he'd been on Will Coop's place for the last two years.

As for Gabriella, she came from a farming background, which always helped. Her father was Bernie Mickleson, owner of the well-known Romney stud Winiata, near Taihape. The stud dated to 1943.

I was learning most of this from Phil while Gabriella was next door, making a brew. Fair enough: Phil was the stock manager and she was the shepherd. Shepherd-cum-cook, I expected.

"So you give the orders, then?" I said, a little tongue in cheek.

Phil smiled. "Well, sort of."

"How do the pair of you really get along?" I pressed. "I mean, it can't be easy living and working together."

"We get along fine." He shrugged. "She has her two dogs, that keeps her out of mischief."

The lady in question entered the room and didn't see the big wink Phil gave me from behind a partly raised hand. "What's he been telling you?" she asked.

"Just that you two get along real well."

"Oh, do we now!" She tossed her blonde head at her husband with mock indignation.

Brian Lloyd and Cloud.

Gabriella and Phil Turner on Okepuha station.

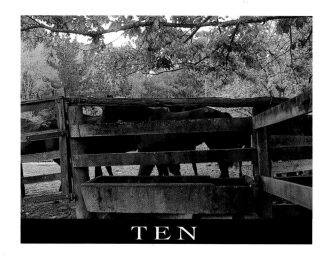

TEN

THE END OF
AN ERA

On Ruangarehu station, Rangi Haraki shook his balaclava-clad head and a heavy frown crossed his features.

"It's bloody sad," he said with deep feeling.

You could say that "bloody sad" best summed up the general feeling on the East Coast when word spread around in the latter part of 1995 that Ihungia, north of Gisborne, very much the station, was about to be sold off.

It was now 10 April 1996, and the new owners of Ihungia, an Asian company called Earnslaw One that was able to meet the asking price of over $6 million, would take control at the end of May. In time, the station I had visited just 17 months previously would become a 5406-hectare pine forest. It was enough to make an East Coast shepherd cringe with apprehension.

If Ihungia had gone under, then where was next?

Rangi Haraki drew a breath. "Makes me feel uncomfortable, y'know. The area's quietened down a lot."

When a station the size of Ihungia closed down there were few in the district who escaped the implications.

He jerked a hand over his shoulder, indicating the nearby Ihungia station complex. "No sheep there now, and the horse sale today. Once the cattle go that'll be it." Again he shook his head. Rangi Haraki was bloody sad, all right.

His slim companion, Mark Williams, looked down in the dumps too. The manager of the 1800-hectare

East Coasters Rangi Haraki and Mark Williams.

*Handling a spooky one: Tony Hansen, behind the horse, and
Tim Rhodes at the time of an earlier visit to Ihungia.*

cattle and horses, and adding the pine trees over the roughest country. The ideal solution in a perfect world.

The horse sale was today and a steady stream of vehicles, most towing horse trailers and churning up dust on the winding, unsealed route off Highway 35 north of Te Puia Springs, passed the woolshed and yards on Ruangarehu and a little further down the road entered Ihungia. At noon would begin the complete dispersal of 104 horses.

These Ihungia-bred horses were not your everyday station hacks of dubious parentage. They could be traced right back to a stallion called Kingston, a real champion the Murphy family imported from Kentucky at around the turn of the century. Ihungia horses had made their mark in showjumping, dressage and endurance trekking, and on the hunting field; any high-country shepherd who rode those steep East Coast hills on a sure-footed Ihungia-bred mount did so with pride.

At the station complex I jostled for parking space as a light drizzle fell. I glanced over to the eight-stand woolshed and the shearers' quarters nearby. There

property was third generation on a place that carried 4250 Marshall Romney ewes and 400 Angus breeding cows. Ruangarehu had once been a part of Ihungia and, Mark reckoned, Puketiti.

He shuffled his boots and fingered his beard before saying, "Hey, I'm not anti-forestry. Certainly there's a place for it. But what I really would've liked to see with Ihungia was a compromise between farming and forestry."

"Along what lines?" I prompted him.

"Oh, say, two parts farming and one part forestry." He turned to Rangi, who nodded his head in agreement. Maori and Pakeha were seeing eye to eye and there was nothing unusual about that on the East Coast.

Perhaps Mark Williams was right: perhaps a compromise was the best way of doing things in the long term. That way they could retain a lot of Ihungia the way it was for over a century, keeping the sheep,

Nearing high noon at Ihungia.

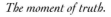

The moment of truth.

would be no more back-breaking hours spent in the woolshed, no more shearing gangs camped in the men's quarters. It was all history now. Almost all of those who'd been there at the time of my last visit were gone, but they, like all the old hands who'd done a season or two on Ihungia, would remember the place. It was a station that carried a great reputation, and it never did anyone's mana any harm to say he'd worked on the place.

For the manager of the station, Tony Hansen, and his Perth-born wife Gaye, it had been the sale of the sheep and their subsequent removal from the station that had made the talk a shattering reality. They had lived on Ihungia for 17 years and had raised four fine boys there. Now they faced an uncertain future.

There would be others who would miss Ihungia: Cooch, the head shepherd, for one. I knew he'd come back to help Tony with the horse muster and subsequent sale and I kept an eye open for him. There must have been 500 people at the station but it would have been hard to miss Cooch, who stood all of 2 metres tall.

The bottom line was that you didn't get people to stay on a property for years unless it was a top place to work. Jack and Edna Cahill, the cowboy/cook combination, had been 13 years on the place and they were still there. The fencer, Robby Broughton, had worked there 10 years and recently

Elders auctioneer David Howarth asks the question.

retired bulldozer driver Darky Taulkamo had been there 38 years – a lifetime. The Williams-owned Ihungia had always been a top place to work on and it was never better than when Tony Hansen was the manager.

My previous visit, at an out-station called Pukeremu, I'd spent some time with Tony and Cooch and the mustering gang. They were a well-drilled team and Tony, while definitely the boss man, didn't come on too strong. In fact, over two days I could not recall Tony raising his voice once, not even when some of the horses they were working with proved difficult, if not downright dangerous, to handle. I reckoned Tony Hansen was the kid of boss most men would have swum a flooded East Coast river for.

With the sale due to start in about 30 minutes, I soaked up the atmosphere, acutely aware of the significance of the day. I had a powerful hunch that on the East Coast they would talk about the sale for a very long time to come. I found a vantage point where I looked down on the stockyards and, over to my right, the old stables.

Prospective buyers mingled with the horses, each of which had a white number on the hip. A booklet gave further details: Lot 19, for example, was a chestnut gelding called Russell; his father was Prospect (purchased by the station from Chris Monckton in 1980 to improve stamina and bone). The horses were apprehensive, constantly moving – perhaps they sensed that their lives would never be the same again. The rain had stopped, but the sky was sullen and there was every indication that it would rain again before too long.

I caught up with tall Cooch – actually Neville – Higgins. He was now the manager on Pouriwai, a 1000-hectare property owned by Gerald Kemp. They ran 4000 Coopworth/Perendale breeding ewes and 250 Charolais/Simmental cattle. For Cooch, an East Coast horseman from way back, it must have seemed very tame stuff after the big, high country of Ihungia, where Hikurangi dominated the skyline.

I indicated the activity around me. "End of an era, Cooch?"

Cooch looked about him. He had been on the station for eight years. How many times, I wondered to myself, had he saddled up his horse at the stables? He looked down from his great height, soft brown eyes pensive under the wide brim of his hat. "Yeah, it's gettin' like that," was all he said.

A few minutes later I spotted a bearded Jack Cahill perched on the top rail of a fence. Unlike Tony, Jack had only a slim chance of getting another similar job. After all, 63 was not a desirable age to be in the employment market.

Jack was not sad about what had happened, he was angry. "You know, I was expecting to work here until I

Julie Kilsby riding Cupid.

was 65 or even a bit older than that. But now" – his face worked – "it seems I've got no choice but to retire." He paused. "No," he finally said, "I'm not at all happy about what's happened here."

For Jack the day-to-day reality of looking after and milking the cows, tending the station garden, killing sheep for cookshop tucker, had become only a memory, things to reflect on as the autumn of his life gave way to early winter.

I moved around a bit, chatting briefly with the East Coast characters. Among them was Ross Buskie, manager on a property near Matawai for 25 years and a dog trialist for longer than that. He had been compiling a photographic record of Ihungia as a working station, but his photographic opportunities were fewer and fewer.

The sale was well underway and the bidding was brisk. Young Julie Kilsby rode an appealing bay gelding into the sale ring. Cupid's father was also Prospect; in Prospect ran the blood of Oklahoma, a horse purchased from Mangaheia station in 1961; Oklahoma could be traced back to Kingston.

As Julie Kilsby, straight-backed, rode around the perimeter of the sale ring, auctioneer David Howarth did his stuff. The bidding stopped at $2600 and Julie rode Cupid out of the ring. Cupid did not belong to Ihungia anymore.

ELEVEN

A WET DAY
ON TANGIHAU

O n a rainswept April morning, Dean McHardy walked casually up to a great lump of a horse and then, quicksilver fast, slipped a halter around its neck. The big horse blew loudly through flared nostrils.

"Captain Dolan," Dean said, introducing me to the resident stallion on Tangihau, a 6100-hectare hill-country property 50-odd kilometres inland from Gisborne. The 33-year-old manager stroked Captain Dolan's velvety muzzle and, in return, the stallion rubbed his hard, bony head against Dean's Swanndri-clad shoulder. Obviously these two were good mates.

Dean McHardy had earned his spurs working on such notable East Coast stations as Waipaoa and Puketiti before arriving to fill the manager's role on

Tangihau in 1990. He lived with his wife Joanne and their three children in a spacious homestead that had the look of the 1920s about it.

Tangihau was yet another station up this way that still used horses and had no intention of dispensing with them. Following my visit to the Ihungia horse sale, that had to be the very best of news. There were around 80 horses here altogether, with 28 of them being brood mares; Captain Dolan was king stud with no pretenders to his throne. Tangihau, ranging in altitude from 200 metres to 630 metres, was ideal horse country, and most of the horses were raised for use on the station. Motorbikes had never been in favour here for stock work – the terrain, broken mudstone country with a pumice overlay, was hell on wheels in the winter when rainfall could be quite excessive.

Dean McHardy filled me in on the proud stallion. "He came from a joker, Bill Dolan – he's a local blacksmith. We've had him for five years now. He's about 19." He ran an appreciative eye over the quietly standing stallion. "He's got the good, strong constitution and easy-going nature of the Clydesdale cross. The boys can actually ride him; we've even used him for packin' out deer from the back."

The manager explained that, as on many North Island stations that had had red deer numbers depleted during the long period of helicopter activity, on Tangihau the deer were "coming back". Red deer, in fact, could sometimes be seen from near the main station complex, up on the top-dressed, grassy hills where stands of native bush had been retained. For that matter, attractive pockets of bush, usually in creek-filled gullies or in basins, could be seen all around the station and they provided deer with excellent habitat.

It was now common for the men to see deer grazing in the open. The best hunting on the place was in a 200-hectare patch of bush that served as a private hunting reserve for station personnel and their friends. In the tail-end of the roar of 1994, Dean had

Dean McHardy and Captain Dolan.

taken a red stag out of there that carried 16 points. While the poor tops attested to the fact that the stag was past his prime, it still added up to a fine trophy.

When Dean removed the halter from Captain Dolan's head and gave him an affectionate flick with it on the rump, the stallion cantered off with a gleeful snort to meet up with a couple of good-looking mares.

Later, out in the middle of the station with the rain still coming down, Dean gave me the stock details. He had it off pat: they carried 20,000 breeding ewes and, as Dean phrased it, "put a Romney ram over a Perendale ewe". They intended to winter 30,000 sheep. A lot of the sheep work was done away from the main station headquarters, out at Tommy's yards, about 12 kilometres from the homestead on a metal road. Tommy's yards was, in effect, an out-station, with accommodation for the men and a five-stand woolshed.

Tangihau was also an Angus stud and had been since 1949. There were 70 breeding cows in the stud and the basic idea was to breed bulls for their commercial herd. They had sold two bulls recently, one for $15,000, the other $10,000. Total cattle numbers were about 2000. Last year, because of the drought, they too had put cattle on the road to graze on other stations.

Kelly Winiata.

They'd taken them as far as Tiniroto, a week's easy ride away. The drovers had camped in a caravan and in shearers' quarters along the way.

Back at the station's nerve-centre, Dean McHardy showed me the singlemen's quarters, and they were well worth showing off. The accommodation could best be likened to a superior motel. The main living room was spacious and the furniture comfortable; a log-burner provided warmth in winter and a large ceiling fan stirred the air in summer. The boys could watch a television when they wanted to. Each of the seven bedrooms had a telephone connection and television aerial socket. There was a washing machine and even a drying room complete with powerful heater.

Dean gestured at the compact kitchen, part of the open-plan arrangement of the main living area. "The boys can cook a feed for themselves at the weekends or if they're running late after rugby practice."

The whole place was neat and clean, but still had a nice homely feel about it. It was so different from the usual station accommodation for singlemen, which, to give an example, could have had three or four rough-as-guts university students staying in it.

Dean McHardy was looking pleased with himself. "Not bad, eh?" He waited for my reaction.

Not bad, I mused as I recalled the old, draughty hut I'd had to make do with on the first sheep station I ever worked on in outback New South Wales. They ran more rats and mice than sheep on that particular place and a good number of those same rats nested and fought and mated inside the thin walls and up in the ceiling of my ratshit accommodation.

"There's only one problem with this place, Dean," I said at last.

His eyebrows shot up. "There is?"

"Yeah, how does a young bloke get used to something else after this?"

The young blokes presently living in the quarters were head shepherd Richard Chrystall and shepherds James Hoole, Peter Bennet and Jason Hammond. Jason had been a cadet at Smedley station when I'd visited it in 1992 and had been at Tangihau for six months. According to Dean, he was shaping up well. There was also a married shepherd on the payroll – Tausy Kingi.

Outside the rain was drizzling.

Richard indicated another building in the complex. "Feel like a brew?"

"Lead on," I replied.

Into the flash cookshop we went, minus boots, of course. The cookshop was the domain of Faith Parkes and had been for seven years. It was bright, airy and immaculate, the best cookshop I'd ever seen on any station. Perhaps it lacked character, but you couldn't develop character in a building as new as this one.

Dean and I sat down at the table with Faith and her husband Charlie, a general hand. Faith seemed a nice, caring type; I wouldn't have minded eating in her cookshop on a regular basis. Also there were fencer Pat Robin and Tony Wanda, but it was the man at the far end of the table who interested me most. Roadman Kelly Winiata was the longest-serving man on the station; hell's teeth, Kelly Winiata was the longest-serving man I

Angus cattle on Tangihau.

had met on any of the stations I had visited.

Kelly's father Jack was a noted shearer in these parts who had come to work at Tangihau when Kelly was a babe in arms.

"When was that?" I asked.

"Dunno, eh? Long time ago . . ."

Kelly was born in 1938, so he must have come to Tangihau in the late thirties or early forties. Kelly Winiata was right: it was a long time ago. All up, he had put in 32 years unbroken service on Tangihau. But then this station, owned by the Bayley and de Lautour families since 1937, was another of those stations where the bosses knew how to treat a hard-working man.

It was still chucking down the wet stuff when, later that day, I thanked Dean McHardy for his help and went on my way. As I headed back to the highway, I thought about Kelly Winiata and the stable life he had led in comparison with mine. At the time he had started at Tangihau, I was a professional hunter with the Forest Service. During that year, I had taken some time off to visit England and my homeland, Wales. Since then, I couldn't count the number of different roofs I had slept under. Working for 32 years on one place was beyond my comprehension.

TWELVE

WILD HORSES ON OHINEWAIRUA

SPRING 1994

With a sweeping gesture Richard Hayes, standing on the highest point of Ohinewairua station, drew my attention to the broad valley of the Aorangi Stream. More a river than a stream, the Aorangi rose to the east of Three Kings Range in the Kaimanawa Mountains and merged not that far from where we stood with the Moawhango River about 25 kilometres north of Taihape. It was wonderful country and I said as much.

Richard Hayes nodded his head. I wondered, but in truth could not again comprehend, what it would be like to stand in such a commanding spot and know that you owned 12,000 hectares of the country around.

On that well-cropped greenery below were toy-like sheep and cattle.

"They're basically Corriedales, a great sheep for the high country," Richard told me. "We winter over 50,000 stock units, and that includes 1000 head of mainly Angus cattle and 900 red deer." He pointed out a collection of buildings. "That's Aorangi out-station."

I noted a big woolshed, cookshop-cum-shearers' quarters, a stand of pine trees that formed a windbreak. The complex was close to the stream, a most agreeable spot. The out-station was less than a 30-minute drive from the main homestead, just off the Napier-Taihape road.

"We spend a fair bit of time out here," Richard went

It is possible the presence of wild horses on Ohinewairua could be traced back to the time of the Land Wars.

on. "You'd think it was Mark's second home at times." Mark, his 33-year-old unmarried son, was the stock manager on the place. Mark was a top horseman and a keen hunter. There was sika deer country not far from the out-station, and in Mark's enviable position, I'd have been camped at the out-station a fair bit too.

When Richard Hayes had taken the station on in 1974 just about all of the country we were looking over was a scrubby wilderness – at least 2400 hectares of it. In such heavy cover wild pigs were rampant; a professional hunter brought in by Richard eliminated 2000 of them. The hunting, combined with a gradual loss of cover as the land was cleared, eventually solved the problem.

Back in 1974 there were huge numbers of red deer on the back reaches of the station. Out there the valley of the Aorangi Stream opened to broken, mesa-like terrain. It was harsh, high-altitude country, often under heavy snow, raked by ferocious winds, and largely unfit for stock. Even before Richard Hayes came to the station the general feeling was that the deer were welcome to it. The red deer that ranged both Ohinewairua and nearby Ngamatea station were arguably the last of the really big North Island herds.

Foot hunters had never been welcome. They left gates open, allowing stock to intermingle. Worse, they sometimes shot stock. They were just plain bad news. Even for deer poachers it was difficult to reach these big herds. The front of their range was blocked off by big stations and at the back there was Army land.

The period of the mid-seventies was the turning point for the deer. Hungry for largely untouched hunting areas, the helicopter hunters discovered the big stations of the Inland Patea. Stations like Ohinewairua, Ngamatea, Otupae and Mangaohane were special targets and the back country of such properties became vast killing grounds. No one knew just how many deer

were killed by helicopter shooters before the deadly one-sided game ended in the late eighties. One thing was certain: the very core of the red deer population had been destroyed.

Wild horses also ranged Ohinewairua. Small numbers of them, pretty much isolated from the main Kaimanawa herds, were found in the harsh and unforgiving country once inhabited by thousands of red deer. Moreover, they were easy to locate once you knew where to look for them.

I had first seen wild horses on the Kaingaroa plains back in 1961 and 1962, and I could not recall seeing any since. What was it about those words – "wild horses" – that moved me so much? Did "wild horses" mean wild country? Did "wild horses" express freedom of spirit, of not being contained?

"Why don't you come back and take a look at them when you can find the time," Richard Hayes suggested. "Mark'll be only too pleased to take you, I expect." He paused. "You could stay at the out-station."

"I'll be back!"

Richard Hayes smiled. "I expect you will at that."

AUTUMN 1995

Wild horses were running on the back of Ohinewairua station, cantering through the rain-soaked tussocks, leaving tell-tale tracks in the claggy ground. They were running free in a high land that might have been theirs.

The first indications that horses ranged the Kaimanawa Mountains appeared on 15 March 1876, when a local runholder, Robert Batley, came across their tracks beyond the headwaters of the Moawhango River. They seemed to have evolved from both military and Maori horses that, one way or another, ended up having to fend for themselves in the central North Island.

Like the Plains Indians of North America the Maoris, when given the opportunity to do so, soon became a race of highly skilled horsemen. The Maoris took to the horse early: Maori Land Records stated that during the 1830s a Danish trader provided horses for the Tuhoe tribe of the Whakatane/Urewera region.

As it happened, it was to the Urewera country that the guerilla leader Te Kooti went in late 1868 or early 1869. The far-reaching bushlands offered Te Kooti a hiding place, and while he was there he set about forming a band of fighting men the equal of any opposition. British and Maori troops combed the Urewera country in pursuit of the rebel, but Te Kooti's followers were many, their eyes ever watchful, their ears ever alert. Te Kooti remained a will-o'-the-wisp.

A warrior such as Te Kooti could only hide for so long, and in June 1869 he and his men left their stronghold. Each of the perhaps 200 men was mounted on a good horse, and each was well armed, many with firearms. The campaign would see Te Kooti involved in hard action both south and north of Lake Taupo.

Te Kooti learnt that there were 14 colonist cavalrymen camped at Opepe, about 20 kilometres south-east of Taupo, who were waiting to be joined by some kupapa (pro-Government Maoris) engaged in the hunt for Te Kooti. Some of Te Kooti's men, posing as the kupapa, entered the Pakeha encampment without raising suspicion, and killed nine of the troopers while suffering no losses. The troopers' horses were either captured or scattered over the Rangitaiki plains.

The elusive Te Kooti continued with his mostly hit-and-run tactics. Three months later, however, he engaged in serious battle with Henare Tomoana and his mostly Maori troops. His victory here was sweet – and

The wild horses were running without sound.

the capture of 100 horses was especially sweet.

Te Kooti's luck ran out late that year when he was defeated in battle west of Turangi. Worse, his priceless horses were abandoned as the rebel leader fled with the remnants of his fighting force to the King Country.

There was no way of knowing just how many horses Te Kooti abandoned in his escape, but a conservative estimate would be well over 100. All of the evidence suggested that the tracks of horses that Owhango runholder Robert Batley came across in the Kaimanawa Mountains could be linked directly with the horses Te Kooti abandoned seven years previously.

A significant personality in New Zealand's early history, Donald McLean, would also play a telling role in the story of the wild horse in this country. The 20-year-old McLean arrived in New Zealand in 1840, and the young Scotsman never looked back in this land of opportunity. He established himself as a land purchaser for the Government and eventually became a Cabinet Minister. In 1858 he took up 3600 hectares of land west of Hastings and this became Maraekakaho station.

Donald McLean was a horseman in a land of horsemen, and in the 1860s he imported a number of Welsh pony brood mares and two Welsh stallions, Comet and Dinarth Caesar. For quite some time McLean had been impressed with the Carlyon breed that his friend Major George Gwavas Carlyon of Gwavas station had developed from an Exmoor stallion mated with locally bred mares. McLean mated mares of Exmoor blood from Gwavas with his Welsh stallion Comet and produced a new breed which he called Comet. Comets were strong, sure-footed, even-tempered animals of sound constitution. Soon they were eagerly sought after for both saddle and harness work.

A wild stallion grazing, photographed with a telephoto lens.

110

In 1876, after Robert Batley's discovery of horse tracks in the Kaimanawa Mountains, Donald McLean liberated an unrecorded number of horses – Exmoor/Welsh crossbred mares and a stallion – on the Kaingaroa plains. Sir Donald McLean died in Napier in January 1877, and so did not see the results of the liberation.

As it turned out, he had selected the horses well. The semi-wild horses still found in the mountains of Wales and in the bleak Exmoor land-scape were true survivors that could be traced right back to the feral horses of pre-historic times. The free-ranging horses found in the Kaimanawa Mountains today, mere remnants of the thousands of wild horses that once ranged the central North Island, still displayed their Welsh/Exmoor blood. They were a tangible link with our history and, as such, were national treasures worthy of protection.

They run Corriedales in the attractive, limestone-rich Ohinewairua country.

the valley of the Aorangi Stream to the Kaimanawa Mountains – would have been memorable. A curtain of mist blanketed the land, a heavy weight you could feel but not touch. It was a place without real colours; we might have been actors in a faded black and white film.

I made a pithy comment about the weather.

Mark smiled. "Shitty, all right." His breathing, unlike mine, was under control. "We'll get on to some horses I saw the other day soon," he added, the smile still in place.

Mark Hayes was soon proven right about that. The wild horses, at least nine of them, were foraging in a high and sheltered basin. All were lovely horses, but by far the most beautiful was a Palomino mare. With her was a foal.

There was a shift in the breeze and the horses got wind of us. The Palomino mare moved first to protect her long-legged foal, then suddenly they

Mark Hayes and I left the Aorangi out-station in the pre-dawn to be greeted by a murky morning. Presently we left the vehicle behind us and, in a light drizzle, started to climb towards an unseen skyline. It was a hard slog.

I was badly disappointed that the weather wasn't better higher up. On a good day the view – clear across

were all running. The horses quickly separated, two of them loping below a rocky bluff partly obscured by wreaths of mist that also muffled the sound of drumming hooves. In a matter of seconds there was only silence as the horses ran without sound, and the Palomino mare and her foal were gobbled up by the mist.

THIRTEEN

FROM STATION TO FARM

Sir Donald McLean's Maraekakaho was very much the station in Hawke's Bay, but under the guiding hand of his son it achieved greatness.

Starting out in 1858 with 3600 hectares of swamp, bracken and scrub, Donald McLean had gradually enlarged the property by purchasing the Maori land and Pakeha farms adjoining it. In 1877 the station passed to his only son Robert. As a young man Robert had played rugby in some of the first matches ever held in New Zealand. On a dare, he had once rode a penny-farthing bicycle from Wellington to Napier over the Rimutaka Hill. After the death of his father, Robert changed the spelling of his surname to MacLean.

Robert continued to buy up land until Maraekakaho covered over 20,000 hectares – it would never be larger in size. Peak sheep numbers – in this period they ran an English Leicester flock – stood at 63,000. There were 80 permanent staff, many of whom came from Scotland – and many of these could not speak English. There were shepherds, cattlemen, ploughmen, gardeners, engineers, butchers, cooks (around 120 loaves were turned out each week in the bakehouse), cowboys, rouseabouts, a bookkeeper and a plumber. When the school was opened in 1893 there was also a schoolteacher. At that time there were about 20 married couples on the station and, of the 11 children who enrolled at the new school, only three had attended school previously.

Quite apart from housing for the managers and their

A Clydesdale stallion on Glenaray station, Southland.

On the Kaiwaka Range.

families, MacLean provided singlemen's quarters, a post office-cum-store, stables and coach houses. Regular dances and other social events, meetings and religious services were held in a big hall, which also contained a 3000-book library for the use of station people and those who lived in the district.

The swaggers' whare was a big roomy hut that provided accommodation for many. A man could turn up with a swag on his back and not a brass farthing in his pocket and be treated right royally on Robert MacLean's station. At the office he was handed a ticket that entitled him to dinner, a bed for the night and breakfast. In the morning he was expected to move on. Station records revealed that in the 1880s as many as 2000 meals were served to swagmen each year.

Everyone ate very well on Maraekakaho station. To provide a change from the usual mutton and beef there were fowl-houses and pig-sties, as well as a large vegetable garden and fruit trees. In a sense, the headquarters of Maraekakaho station formed a small township in itself. Not all of the staff, however, lived there – a good many were based at out-stations.

Part of the big run, an area of drained swampland, was called The Valley. Out here was a big stud farm where Merino, English Leicester and Lincoln sheep studs had been established. There was a Shorthorn cattle stud as well as a Clydesdale horse stud, not forgetting Major Carlyon's ponies of Exmoor blood and the Comet breed of horse, now at the peak of its popularity.

The main woolshed and yards were at the station headquarters. Rated among the biggest in the land, they could hold 5000 sheep overnight. In about 1910 the woolshed became one of the first in the country to have shearing machines. There were 28 shearing stands: two long boards of 14 stands facing each other. One board was for the Maori shearers and one board for the Pakehas, and each morning the scene was set for serious competition. After work a large crowd of onlookers invariably turned up at the woolshed to hear each shearer's tally called out. The woolclip was taken by bullock dray to Clive, a three-day trip. From there it was taken on surfboats to sailing vessels that serviced all of the East Coast.

The sheep found at Maraekakaho were by any standards outstanding. They won numerous prizes at New Zealand A & P Shows and events in Australia. The station's wool exhibit was taken to such prestigious events as the Paris Exhibition of 1889, where it won a gold medal, and three years later to the Chicago World's Fair, where it was awarded the coveted Medal of Honour.

In the early 1890s the Government brought in a heavy land tax and as a result of this many properties were reduced in size. At the time about 2400 hectares of Maraekakaho was sold off in two blocks, and more land was sold as the years went by until – in 1912 – the station was reduced to 4900 hectares.

In 1927 Robert MacLean was, like his father before him, knighted but, again like his father, he did not enjoy his knighthood for long. He died two years later.

Following the death of Sir Robert MacLean the

Kowhai in mid-spring.

vultures moved in and in 1930 the property was subdivided and sold by auction. The 20,000 hectares that had made up Maraekakaho at its peak were now split between over 60 farms. Sir Donald McLean would not have approved.

Brilliant sunshine came with Easter Monday.

On the top of the Kaiwaka Range – low-lying hills about 30 kilometres north of Napier – an unusual breed of cattle were grazing. I had stopped my vehicle to observe them and, leaning against the fence, I watched them for several minutes. The cattle were South Devons, a breed invariably associated with farm-sized properties, not stations.

As at Maraekakaho, the once large Hawke's Bay station of Tutira had been gradually reduced to nothing like its former glory. At its peak Tutira was around 24,000 hectares and upon that land they ran 38,000 sheep. In size and stock numbers it was not unlike Maraekakaho, but there all similarity ended. Tutira at its best was never the elaborate showplace that Maraekakaho undoubtedly was.

Tutira's size was gradually eroded, first when the lease of Maori land ran out and later when some of the remaining land was subdivided for settlement by soldiers returning from the First World War. Among the returned soldiers was Joseph Turnbull, who took up one of the eight or so sections of the Kaiwaka Soldiers' Settlement.

As a boy, Joseph Turnbull lived in Christchurch. So did Eva Hampton. They went to the same primary school and played together. When Eva was 16 her father David, upon hearing that the big North Canterbury estate of Culverden was to be cut up in the aftermath of the Boer War, decided to enter the ballot. David Hampton won the lottery and the 1200-hectare homestead block, complete with grand manor house, was his.

Joseph Turnbull set off for the war in Europe, was badly wounded at Gallipoli and returned home. He was admitted to Christchurch Hospital and then to a Red Cross convalescent home at Hanmer Springs. Among the voluntary nurses who were working at this convalescent home was none other than Joseph's childhood friend Eva Hampton.

The returned soldiers were encouraged to take up land, either new blocks in virgin bush country or subdivided station country – either way, it was a golden opportunity for a man to make something of himself. Most of the land up for grabs was in the North Island and Joseph went there courtesy of the Government. He heard that a big block of land north of Napier about to be auctioned off was well worth considering. The block in question was, of course, the Kaiwaka, a prime slice of Tutira, sun-drenched and lovely.

What Joseph knew about Hawke's Bay could have been written on the back of a postage stamp, but that didn't stop him putting his name in the ballot. He was among the lucky ones and a 325-hectare block of prime land was transferred to his name.

Joseph's block was 8 kilometres west of the top of the Devils Elbow, a notoriously tortuous section of road south of Lake Tutira on State Highway 2. There was no road access to the tangle of scrub and fern: all supplies were taken into the block by packhorse or bullock-drawn sledge. It would be four years before a vehicle road reached the property. While he built a house, Joseph lived in a tent. When finished the house would become home to Eva, too, because by now they were engaged to be married.

It was spring in Napier when Eva (now Mrs Turnbull) arrived and made the trip to the property for the first time. "When we got to Westshore," she would recall late in life, "my husband pointed out a stand of kowhai trees on the horizon, they seemed so very far away, but that was our destination." The sight of these distant kowhai trees, a splash of brilliant yellow on the skyline, would inspire the Turnbulls to call their property Kowhai Downs.

"We had to make our own fun in those days. I used to play the piano at community functions, whether it was a dance or a farewell for the boys going to the Second World War." In time a nine-hole golf course was built on Kowhai. "Wednesday was ladies' day. The women used to ride around the course on horseback with their clubs thrown over their shoulders. Saturday was set aside for the whole family."

Eva Turnbull, a life member of the Women's Division of Federated Farmers and a member of the Hawke's Bay Women's Club, would say on the celebration of her 90th birthday in 1982: "I have seen great changes, from days of transportation by horses to men walking on the moon. I have seen a property developed from a treeless, unfenced, pumicy waste covered in scrub and fern to a fully developed farm . . . Yes, I feel some sense of achievement."

April was entirely the wrong time of the year for me to see the bright yellow flowers of the kowhai tree; instead I was looking with much interest at the South Devon cattle, so sleek of coat. Wide-eyed, they appeared just as interested in me. I moved further along the fenceline, the better to photograph one in particular, and the main bunch followed me, as aggressive as day-old rabbits.

A signpost in the paddock caught my eye: WEST HAM SOUTH DEVONS. It was a stud farm, then. I wondered who owned it and decided there was only one way to find out.

It was morning tea time – and not smoko – at the home of Stewart and Denise Bradley. They seemed not at all put out by my uninvited knock on the door: they were used to people dropping in unexpectedly. It happened all the time in the country.

The Bradleys, I soon discovered, had purchased their once 235-hectare returned soldier's farm in 1990. They were West Coasters and had brought their 180 head of South Devon cattle with them. The stud, which bred bulls for the commercial market, had been established on the West Coast in the early 1980s. I didn't have to be

told that Hawke's Bay, being considerably more central, made far more sense as a location than the more isolated West Coast. At the moment, their 21-year-old son Dave was up in Auckland displaying their cattle at the Easter Show.

I asked Stewart why they had chosen the breed, and he explained that the beasts had a marvellous temperament – in fact, the South Devon was the greatest thing he had ever farmed.

Stored away in my memory with heaps of other information I might never use was a fact about the South Devon. "Aren't they known as 'Gentle Giants'?" I asked.

Stewart nodded his head.

The South Devon was considered the largest of the British breeds, and a bull would stand about 155 centimetres at the withers and weigh approximately 1250 kilograms. South Devons were originally developed as draught animals, but they were now raised for their beef, which was known for both its tenderness and its texture. They shared blood with the zebu, a humped ox found in Africa and Asia, and this apparently accounted for their ability to withstand tropical climates.

Stewart Bradley finished his tea, pushed back his chair and stood up, informing me that he'd like me to see something interesting down at the yards. On the way down there he enlightened me still further about South Devons. They were, he said, just about unheard of in New Zealand 30 years ago, but now the South Devon Society (of New Zealand) had 120 members all over the country.

Down at the wooden-railed yards there was a six-month-old South Devon calf. It was in great condition, and Stewart, fixing a halter to its head, was obviously proud of it.

"It's not been weaned yet," he said. "We're going to show it soon. It weighs around 450 kilograms."

Stewart Bradley displays with pride a six-month-old South Devon calf.

"Fast growth," I said, impressed.

Stewart nodded. "A Hereford calf would weigh about 350 or 380 kilograms at the same age."

"Okay if I touch it?"

"Sure," Stewart said. "No worries."

I rubbed the calf's forehead and, had it been a kitten, it might have purred. It was another Gentle Giant in the making.

Looking over the cultivated land that was once Kakariki station, it required imagination to visualise it as it once was – fern, manuka, scrub – a wild pig's haven. It took even greater vision to conceive that it was here, in this most peaceful of scenes, that a Scotsman called David Balfour lived in fear of his life for several years.

Maungaharuru station, some 8000 hectares of wild Mohaka River country, was a place of precipitous cliffs, difficult of access and difficult to farm. The station dated to about 1859, when Philip Dolbel had taken up the lease, but by all accounts Dolbel, not on good terms with the local Maoris, did very little with his land. In 1868, perhaps short of funds, he sold 4000 hectares of it to David Balfour, who was married to Dolbel's niece, and George Farrow. Both were working on W.T. Guinness's Moeangiangi station at the time, Balfour as manager and Farrow as shepherd.

Together, then, Balfour and Farrow ran a few sheep on their block, which they named Kakariki after the parakeet. They fenced off a small paddock for a garden and decided where to build a homestead. And all the while they continued to work on Moeangiangi station on a casual basis.

Meantime, Te Kooti, entrenched in his vast Urewera stronghold, was proving more than troublesome. It was a time of lightning-fast raids, of tomahawk and fire, of split skulls and burnt homesteads. No one who opposed Te Kooti felt safe. In later life, David Balfour would recall that for about four years he never slept on Kakariki without a loaded rifle to hand.

In April 1869 Te Kooti heard that the nearby settlement of Mohaka, the home of a hapu that was hostile to him as well as a store of government ammunition, was largely unguarded. Te Kooti moved fast. En route to Mohaka the rebel band came to Springhill station.

John Lavin owned the 4000-hectare Springhill station, upon which he ran mostly cattle. The station was about 10 kilometres upriver of the Mohaka settlement, and the homestead stood about 150 metres from the river. Te Kooti's men came via the river and Lavin, his wife, their three young sons, a man called Cooper who had come to warn them of possible attack, and an old man who worked as a cowboy on the place were all killed.

No mercy was shown by Te Kooti at the Mohaka settlement either. Here 57 Maoris and seven Europeans, including many women and children, were butchered. Te Kooti lost about a dozen men. The dead, friend and foe, were left to rot where they had fallen when Te Kooti's band put the settlement behind them. They returned to the mountains killing, looting and burning as they went.

Two days would pass before David Balfour and several others reached the Mohaka settlement. When they did, the stench of dead bodies was stomach-turning. They buried those they had known, Pakeha and Maori alike, but Te Kooti's men received no such treatment. They were either left where they were or simply dragged by a leg to a high cliff overlooking the river and hurled into it.

The Lavins had been very good friends of David Balfour and George Farrow's, and their horrific deaths were a chilling reminder of what could happen to families on outlying stations. For Farrow it was all too much: he wanted out, and fast. He offered his share of the station to his partner. David Balfour had also had a gutsful of rebellious Maoris, but it wasn't in his nature to quit. He turned to Philip Dolbel for financial help and soon became the sole owner of Kakariki.

For the rest of his time on the station, David Balfour lived in constant fear of Maori attack. The last straw came in early 1872 when a splinter group of Te Kooti's Urewera Hauhaus raided Philip Dolbel's Maungaharuru station. No lives were lost in the brief skirmish, but the homestead and woolshed were burnt to the ground. From then on David Balfour was determined to leave the Mohaka district. In August 1872 he sold the Kakariki lease to George and Frank Bee and took up the job of manager on Gwavas station. He most likely slept much better there.

For the 20 years they held Kakariki, the Bee family had a peaceful time of it. Following their departure in 1892 the station had a series of owners, until in 1915 the property came back into the hands of the Bee family when the two sons of George and Frank purchased it. By this time the station stood at 7300 hectares. They ran 14,000 sheep on cultivated land and the woolclip was 200 bales in a good year. At least half of the station, however, was unbroken country where wild horses and feral cattle, pigs and Merinos ruled.

The earthquake of 1931 caused massive damage on Kakariki, both to the station buildings and the land, and this may well have been the reason why that year the Bee family sold the station to the Government. Kakariki was reduced in size in 1953 when three farm-sized blocks were put up for ballot, and it was further diminished in 1961 when six more farms were established.

The Mohaka River near Mohaka.

Vance Percy, astride a farmbike, throttled back to a halt. With the engine ticking over smoothly, he gazed with the pride of ownership across green pastures to where some of his cattle were grazing.

The land we stood on was once Kakariki station, but today it was a 300-hectare farm. In 1953 Vance's father Bill had paid £10 an acre (£25 a hectare) for it and considered it a bargain. Many years on, Vance Percy ran about 100 Santa Gertrudis cross cows in partnership with his father, and 30 Santa Gertrudis stud cows in partnership with his wife Denise. Their top Santa Gertrudis bull Tintagel Largo was imported from Australia in 1985.

Vance Percy considered that the Santa Gertrudis breed was at the same stage in this country today as it was some 30 years ago in Australia. He ought to know – he spent five years working with the breed on two top studs in New South Wales and Queensland.

The first Santa Gertrudis cattle imported into Australia arrived in 1932. They were greeted by local cattlemen with open scorn, who reckoned they were much too "exotic" a breed to ever take on. It wasn't until the King Ranch of Texas moved into the Australian scene in the early fifties, bringing their Santa Gertrudis cattle with them, that a real impact was made. By the nineties Santa Gertrudis cattle made up a large part of the Australian beef industry. World-wide they were found in 45 countries.

Vance Percy looks over some of his cattle.

As Vance Percy pointed out, the breed was becoming more popular in New Zealand, and it was not difficult to understand why. The Santa Gertrudis was considered a large beef breed: a mature bull weighed upwards of 900 kilograms and a mature cow 630–725 kilograms. They were adaptable to a broad range of climatic conditions, including both the steamy heat of Australia's far north and the more temperate conditions of New Zealand. They positively thrived on the sparse pickings of a dry summer in Hawke's Bay. They also had exceptional longevity, few problems with calving and heavier calves at weaning, and the beef was known for its tenderness and palatability.

So there I was on a glorious Hawke's Bay afternoon looking at some of the Percys' Santa Gertrudis cattle. They were fine-looking animals, sleek as seals, cherry red in colour. In no way did they look out of place in a Hawke's Bay landscape.

My eyes were drawn beyond the cattle, well beyond the cattle, to the sea. I estimated that the sparkling expanse of ocean was just a little bit south of the place the Mohaka River ended its journey. Once, long ago, I might from this very point have seen a big coastal steamship anchored out there, waiting for a surfboat to bring out the Kakariki woolclip and then transport it down the coast.

Santa Gertrudis cattle.

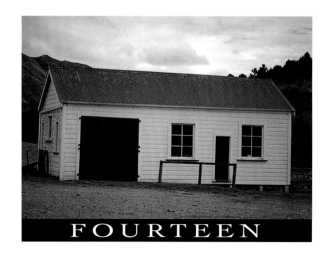

FOURTEEN

THE DUNCAN LEGACY

The out-station on Otairi dated to the late 1930s. It consisted of an eight-stand woolshed and both shearers' and shepherds' accommodation. Located about 12 kilometres from the main station complex, it was named Mangapapa on account of a small river that bisected steep hills at the northern end of the station. To many, however, it was simply called the back woolshed.

On an overcast day, I was at the out-station in the company of Ken Duncan. In his early thirties, Ken was dark and quietly spoken. He wasn't overly talkative and I had a feeling that long and meaningful silences were a part of his usual demeanour. He drew deeply on a smoke he'd made himself and told me that they usually spent about two weeks out here at the main shearing time.

Today Ken and his brother Doug owned the station between them. Neither man lived on the property: Ken had a farm near Otairi and Doug farmed near Marton. They were, however, very much involved in the day-to-day running of Otairi. There was history here: from the time local Maoris sold the land in 1881, the property had never been anything but Duncan-owned.

Among the passengers to arrive at Port Nicholson on the S.S. *Bengal Merchant* in February 1840 were Andrew and Margaret Duncan, and their two sons John, aged three, and Andrew junior, who was just one year old. They had emigrated to New Zealand as a part

Ken Duncan out at the back woolshed.

124

*Inside the woolshed, which dates to the early 1900s
and can hold around 3000 sheep.*

of the New Zealand Company's scheme.

Following a voyage of 103 days, they came ashore to find only a few native huts and makeshift dwellings scattered along the foreshore. Worse, the blocks of rural land the Duncans and others had bought and paid for before leaving Home were not theirs for the taking – survey work was held up while Ngati Toa disputed the sale of the land, and it would be years before the matter was sorted out to everyone's satisfaction.

That year the New Zealand Company acquired 16,000 hectares of land near the mouth of the Wanganui River and a settlement was established. In late 1841 the Duncans moved to this new settlement, called Petre (in 1854 renamed Wanganui), and started a small farm. They prospered.

Time passed. While John Duncan's main interest in life would always be the land, Andrew junior's inclination was to study law. In 1866 John, in his late twenties, married Catherine, the daughter of Richard and Amelia Hammond. They would have three sons: William McAlpin, born 1868; John Hugh, born 1870; and Thomas Andrew, born 1873.

The Hammonds came from Yorkshire in 1844. They settled in the Rangitikei district and named their property York Farm. Catherine Hammond's three brothers were all fine horsemen, and, as can be seen in this extract from Sir James Wilson's *Early Rangitikei*, they enjoyed working cattle.

Mr Richard Hammond's sons, Thomas, William and John, were considered great men with cattle, especially Bill. They leased land all up the river from the Maoris and had cattle running along the river banks, where they readily fattened. Shortly after I came I remember one hundred head being sold to Mr Gear at eleven pounds a head, all fattened along the river, and it must have been an exciting time getting them in, for cattle got very wild in those days. The way the Hammond boys were able to get cattle out of the bush was proverbial and with a pack of dogs and a stock whip, they roamed the bush and seldom were beaten. The marvel is that they were not drowned for they were continually crossing the river when going to their upper run, but Bill did most of the work, he had a charmed life, and, although wet for days and after many escapes, he died only a year ago. He hunted the hounds when they first started in the Rangitikei and no fence was too big for him – he always got over somehow.

During the mid-to-late 1870s local tribal leaders approached the Government with a view to selling a large block of land between the upper reaches of the Rangitikei and Turakina Rivers that they called Otairi. This region was largely unexplored by Pakehas. The Government was lukewarm about the idea, and the Maoris decided to seek a purchaser elsewhere.

By this time John Duncan was as well respected in the Rangitikei district as he was in and around Wanganui. He and his brother, a solicitor since the late 1860s, had, like the Hammond family, always been fair in their dealings with the Maoris. Moreover, it did a great deal for the mana of John Duncan that he spoke fluent Maori.

Would, the Maoris wondered, John Duncan be interested in the block of land called Otairi? To approach him they sent a senior chief, Piripi Te Aokapurangi. He was known to be a man of high principles. The brothers listened intently while Piripi described the land in question. It was mostly in heavy forest; there were many streams and rivers; and wild cattle and pigs were commonplace. Truly there was no better country to be had in the North Island.

The brothers considered. They had heard enough to know the land was suitable for farming on a grand scale, but the asking price was high. Neither brother was given to hasty decisions, but Piripi was in no mood for delays and demanded an immediate response. Young William Duncan recorded the event in his diary: "My father relied absolutely upon the word of Piripi and his confidence was not misplaced. Then and there a bargain was struck and the Chief returned to his people to make arrangements for the completion of the sale."

The Otairi Purchase, as it became known, was finalised in 1881 at a pa on the outskirts of Marton. Three drays had been required to transport the trade goods, part of the purchase price, from Wanganui. These included axes, knives, blankets, flour, sugar and tea.

At nine o'clock in the morning John Duncan stood up to address the 200-strong gathering, which included seven chiefs. John Duncan expounded in Maori on what those present already knew: that the price he and his brother had agreed to was £9000 in cash and trade. To a man the Maoris considered this to be a very generous sum and, in comparison with most Maori land sales, it undoubtedly was. The trade goods were placed in seven equal heaps, while Andrew held the seven parcels of cash. When each chief came forward to collect his share of the proceeds he signed a deed of sale. When the long ceremony was over a meal of wild pork, potatoes and native pigeon was served up. Upon their departure, the Duncans were given a rousing farewell.

A few weeks later Piripi took John Duncan on a tour of inspection of the Otairi block, an area in excess of 10,000 hectares. Such was the density of the forest that most of the time they were on foot, leading their horses. Here stood totara, rimu, miro and matai. John Duncan was most impressed with his land: it was all Piripi had said it was and more. True, the task they faced in clearing it was of Herculean proportions, but it was only a question of time and money and a day-by-day, acre-by-acre attitude.

Felling on Otairi began in late 1881 when John Duncan arrived there for a second time with two skilled bushmen, and in that first year 40 hectares were cleared. More men were hired. They were not difficult to find: the Taihape region was a mecca for bushmen seeking work. The so-called bushwhackers were paid 30 shillings for each acre (75 shillings for each hectare) they cleared. They lived under canvas and, later on Otairi, in whares. Their basic supplies were brought in by packhorse from Wanganui, a two-day trip, 70-odd kilometres of rough bush tracks. They took advantage of what the land offered: it was no problem to get a feed of wild pork or butter-fat native pigeon. Such men were soon clearing around 250 hectares a year on the fledgling station.

Young William Duncan left Wanganui Boys High School when he was 15 and went to work on the station. His father paid him 10 shillings a week to begin with; later Thomas joined his brother at Otairi. It was not clear if their brother John Hugh worked there too, but he was certainly often at the station helping out or off pig hunting.

The big burn-offs were usually done in the autumn, when the prevailing winds would contain such big fires. Once the fallen forest giants and all of the debris had been burnt to ashes, the young Duncan boys pitched in to help sow the cleared land with grass. Men and boys, working in line and each with a sack of grass seed over his shoulder, spread the tiny beginnings of new life over the ash-covered ground and, in doing so, changed the face of the land forever.

Lacking fences at first, the Duncans ran cattle, which could pretty much fend for themselves. They proved a sound investment – a good number of young steers

purchased for a pound each in 1866 sold for more than five times that two years later.

It was John Duncan's intention that his three sons would inherit Otairi when he died, but his plans were thwarted when in 1892, while on a pig hunting expedition, John Hugh Duncan was drowned in the Turakina River. He had tried to cross the rampant floodwaters by hanging onto his horse's tail but, mid-river, they had become separated.

When John Duncan senior passed away in 1906 William and Thomas took over the reins; three years later they split the station between them. Thomas had married Jeannie Priscilla in 1896 and they now had six children. A few years later William Duncan sold off his land (much of which ended up in Thomas's hands later on).

From this point on, Thomas, usually known now as T.A. Duncan, really came into his own. The land that his father had taken up could not have been in better hands. By 1911 tree-felling was a thing of the past on the station. The land had been tamed, although its spirit, beyond the reach of man, would never be broken.

Large-scale fencing and extensive top-dressing by hand were the priorities. They were running 30,000 Romney sheep and 200 head of cattle. At peak times there were as many as 50 men on the payroll, as many as 80 dogs to be fed. The station headquarters was more a village than anything else.

For those men and their families the atmosphere was generally happy. A newspaper reporter visiting Otairi in about 1912 was told by one of the shepherds that "some of the chaps have been here for years, you're treated like the best!"

You didn't have to work on Otairi to be treated well. The hospitality of the early runholders, most evident in the big-run country of the South Island, was alive and well on Otairi in a period when droving was commonplace. The poetic words that follow on page

130, written by an anonymous drover, related to the period just before the First World War.

From 1900 onwards Otairi had sent regular consignments of cattle and sheep to the Gear Meat Works at Petone. The expansion of the meat industry during the First World War was enormous, and the trend continued into the 1920s. From about 1921 onwards New Zealand exported 10 million carcasses of mutton and lamb and 800,000 quarters of beef annually to Britain.

By the late 1920s and for some years thereafter, Otairi climbed on the lucrative export band-wagon. They had an order from Gear Meat to supply them with a staggering 2000 wethers each week from mid-January through to the end of April. Each week 2000 hog-fat sheep were mustered and brought to the main holding yards. From there they were driven to Hunterville, which called for an overnight stop midway, and then on to the railway station, where 30 trucks were required to take them to Petone. They were great days on Otairi.

The most prestigious person to sign the visitor's book at the now famous Otairi station prior to the Second World War was the Duke of Gloucester. During his two-day visit in January 1935 the Duke expressed much interest in shearing and consequently was taken to a woolshed. Thomas Duncan drew the Duke's attention to one shearer in particular, Cyril Bothwick. The plain-talking Bothwick was a top man in any bunch of shearers and today, as usual, he was shearing faster and cleaner than anyone else.

The Duke stepped closer and asked Bothwick how many sheep could he shear in an hour.

Bothwick paused. Then, with a lift of his sweaty shoulders, he replied, "Oh, I dunno . . . I count the first three or four and after that it's just a string of arseholes going through the porthole."

Another incident that caused much merriment on the station happened one blazing hot summer's day when Thomas Duncan was taking his daily ride around the property. The boss rode a big white horse, so he was easy to spot from a distance, and the bush telegraph was usually able to provide information about his route each day.

On this particular day, however, word hadn't reached one shepherd – when Thomas came upon him the man was flat on his back, snoring. At length Thomas considered him. No matter how hot it was there was no excuse for this type of thing. But perhaps there was a better way of teaching the man a lesson than simply bawling him out.

Someone has to repair flood-damaged fencing and here it's the lot of Mark Lawry (left) and Gary Austin.

Romneys range a land cleared of forest.

A RECOGNITION

I've been droving when the weather was both boisterous and cold,
And likewise when the sun was like a ball of molten gold.
In the gloomy days of winter, I've been driving on the track;
Also when the sun was blazing till my skin was like to crack.
I have felt fatigue and hunger, while I've driven weary sheep
Where people would begrudge a bit for man or beast to eat.
But I lately went a-droving, past a station I could name,
Where the river had got flooded by the recent heavy rain.
I was baulked and in a muddle, I was puzzled what to do.
I had come a weary distance, and my sheep were starving too.
I pulled up at the station in a doubtful kind of way
For I knew that they were bothered with intruders every day.
It was also crutching season, so their grass could not be flush
And their yards were very apt to be knee deep in mud and slush.
But I had to face the music and must chance it so to speak
Though I felt like an intruder who was travelling on the sneak.
But my fears were quickly banished, and I felt I need not quail,
As I heard the welcome echoes of a very friendly hail.
Someone sang out "Dinner's ready! Come along, you're just in time."
And just a minute afterwards a bell began to chime.
I had a hearty dinner, my sheep were grazing too,
For I left them in a paddock that the highway passes through.
Then I loitered round till evening, when the bosses hove in sight,
For I meant to humbly ask them if they'd let me stay the night.
So I told them my situation, and, answering with a laugh,
They told me I was welcome, amidst banter fun and chaff.
I wasn't ordered onward, but made welcome there instead
To the very best of eating and a warm, cosy bed.
And grass – my sheep were given the best pasture that they had.
It saved the life of many that were looking weak and bad.
I was treated with a kindness I had seldom met before.
Had I been a wealthy squatter they could have done no more.
Twas the old Otairi Station, and my thanks I freely give
To its owners, whom I'll think of for the longest day I live.
May they always have the power to be generous and free
With their kindly hospitality, just as they were to me.

130

Heading out: Simon Perry (left), Gavin Guineven and Damion Dixon, overleaf: Simon Perry.

When the shepherd woke up it was to the biggest shock of his life. The boss was lying next to him fast asleep. When Thomas awoke, the shepherd was gone.

Of all the Duncans it was Thomas Andrew Duncan who most clearly made his mark. A founder member of the Meat Board in 1922, he later became its chairman. In 1951 he was knighted, and he later established the Sir Thomas and Lady Duncan Hospital in Wanganui for the care and rehabilitation of polio victims. The great man died in 1960 at the age of 87.

The present-day owners of Otairi, the current holders of the legacy, were his great-grandsons.

Like a cardboard cut-out, a horseman was dramatically outlined on a razorback ridge. Half standing in his stirrup irons, he looked towards a well-ordered procession of Romney sheep moving with sure steps around a steep hillface. Behind the sheep his dogs worked with unbridled enthusiasm, more than earning their daily keep.

"Wayleggo!" His voice rang out loud and clear as he called his dogs off.

Earlier on Ken Duncan and I had caught up with the station's three-strong team of shepherds as they headed out from the station after lunch. Capable-looking types with ready laughs, they had drawn rein and exchanged pleasantries. Ken Duncan had seemed perfectly at ease with them, and they with him – Otairi was still the great place to work on that it had always been.

The dogs – huntaways and heading – had milled about the horses' hooves as though they'd just been released after a six-month stretch in a canine prison. The prospect of being on the hill was enough to turn a station dog's mood from pure gloom to sheer ecstasy in the time it took to pull a bolt and open the cage.

Behind the silhouetted Simon Perry the sky was sullen. It had been raining, and it would soon rain again. The Mangapapa River would run high, the Turakina even higher. This was the wrong side of the island for a real drought.

Leaning back casually against the cabin of his vehicle, Ken fished into a shirt pocket and took out a yellow packet. Time for another smoke. He thumbed back the brim of his brown leather hat.

With a gesture, I indicated Simon Perry. "Looks good, doesn't he?"

Ken looked up, then nodded. "Yeah," he said with a half smile. He went on making his cigarette. Once most shepherds smoked, but few did today.

"What's happening exactly?" I asked.

With a quick twirl of his dextrous fingers, Ken turned tobacco and paper into a thin, neat cylinder. He studied it for a moment before lighting up. At last he replied. "The boys are working a 1000-acre paddock, moving all the ewes together, bunching them up for the rams. There are 2500 ewes in the paddock and we work on a one-to-70 ratio – one ram for every 70 ewes." He paused. "That's 35 rams," he said, in answer to my unasked question. He made a sweeping movement. "We keep them together for six weeks."

Still Simon Perry was outlined high above us. He might have epitomised all of the untold numbers of shepherds and stockmen who had ridden over cleared land where long ago trees stood tall and proud and wild pigs foraged on whatever they could find in the sun-splotched ferns beneath.

Suddenly man and horse dropped off the skyline, gone like a puff of smoke from the chimney of an old boundary rider's hut.

The great-grandson of Thomas Andrew Duncan ground the last of his cigarette under a boot heel. "Okay?"

"Sure."

On the move again.

Overleaf: Merinos on Bendigo Station, Central Otago.

FLAXBOURNE

Wairau River

BLENHEIM

Upbrooke

Awatere River

SEDDON

Lake Grassmere

Cape Campbell

Flaxbourne River

Flaxbourne
(1905 – 1996)

Upcot

Lake Elleswater

The Homestead

WARD

Weld Cone

Site of Wards 1847 house

Molesworth

The Muller

Awatere River

Inland Kaikouras

WHARANUI

Barefell Pass

Guide River

Clarence River

Clarence River

Seaward Kaikouras

THE FIRST GREAT SHEEP STATION
IN THE SOUTH ISLAND

FIFTEEN

ON GOLDEN MARLBOROUGH HILLS

The Merino sheep were dotted on the golden Marlborough hills like confetti at a wedding; the sky beyond them was unusually dark, a blue-black. These tussock grasslands, burnished by the last rays of the autumn sun, were once part of the first great sheep station in the South Island: Flaxbourne.

When in 1844 Charles Clifford, Frederick Weld, William Vavasour and Henry Petre took Merino sheep into the Wairarapa via the coastal route and established Wharekaka, the first sheep station in New Zealand, they bit off more than they could chew.

The four men were all upper-class Roman Catholics educated at England's leading Jesuit college, Stonyhurst, in Lancashire. They did not come from a farming background, but they had enough sense to hire Tom Caverhill to run the station. Wharekaka, however, was not all they hoped it would be.

The station's far-reaching swamplands were not the right place to run Merinos – or, for that matter, any other breed. Merinos were particularly prone to footrot and too much rain did not suit their temperament at all. Caverhill's answer was to run the Merinos on the only block of high, dry ground, and the result was that they had a very limited range. The sheep were given a hard time by wild dogs and rampant wild pigs, so Caverhill

On golden Marlborough hills.

136

had the flock guarded by armed shepherds during the day and yarded at night.

Life might have been tough for the sheep, but it was just as tough for the men. The rough homestead was flooded out several times, and the swamps were riddled with mosquitoes. The aristocratic and somewhat genteel Weld later had this to say about the mosquitoes: "No pen can describe, or mind conceive, the horror of them. They put out the wick in a tin of fat, our only lamp. They got into our mouths while eating; they filled the air with their hateful humming." Access to Wellington, even though a pack track had been formed over the Rimutaka Range, was still difficult. Nor did it help matters that the Maoris were demanding more money on the leases.

In about 1846 Vavasour and Petre, always absentee owners, decided to pull out of the Wharekaka venture. At this time Clifford (who would never live on any of his pastoral holdings) was a land agent in Wellington, so it was only Weld who lived at the station with Caverhill and several shepherds.

Frederick Weld was 23 years of age in May 1846; his cousin Charles Clifford was 10 years older and would always be regarded as the senior partner. Despite the inauspicious start, the Clifford-Weld combination, with Clifford's business acumen and Weld's boundless

Where the Mukamuka stream enters Palliser Bay. By this route sheep were first taken into the Wairarapa in 1844.

enthusiasm, would eventually be ranked as one of the most successful pastoral partnerships in early colonial New Zealand.

By mid-1846 Weld had met an ex-whaler called John Stenton Workman. He was married to a local woman and lived in a Maori fishing village at Palliser Bay. Workman had, with his Maori relatives, made many a trip across the straits to catch ducks at two lakes (later Marlborough's Grassmere and Elterwater).

Workman described to Weld a vast, empty place of dry, hilly country running from coast to mountain. The adventurous Weld was fired with a great desire to see this place for himself. For some time now the owners of Wharekaka had talked about expanding their pastoral interests. After all, no fortunes would be made at Wharekaka: Caverhill estimated that at best its stock-carrying capacity was 3000 sheep.

Weld wasted little time in conveying what Workman had told him to his partner. Clifford was typically cautious: he wanted a second opinion of the land. He sought out John Wade, a merchant with shares in several whaling stations in the area in question. They met at Barrett's Hotel (since 1840 the meeting place in Wellington), and Wade's description of the country matched Workman's very well.

Clifford was aware that it was only a matter of time

before settlers would lay claim to the mountainous land across Cook Strait. Certainly whatever good grazing land there was in the area that would later be named Marlborough would soon be snapped up. He and Frederick needed to act with all haste.

Clifford hired Wade, who had a little six-tonne cutter at his disposal, to take Weld and Caverhill on a tour of inspection of their proposed sheep station. On 24 September 1846, the *Fidele* set sail and a day later she was lying off Cape Campbell. In a leather notebook Weld wrote, "As we followed down the coast we observed nothing but low grazing hills until about ten miles from Cape Campbell we came to the mouth of a little river which is marked by a conical peak and one or two hills white with limestone." This "conical peak" stood 368 metres and became known as Weld Cone. The "little river" was the Flaxbourne.

On 26 September Weld noted in his diary:

We entered the estuary where there was six to seven feet [1.8 to 2 metres] of water at low tide and then wishing to place the boat in a more completely land locked position we entered the river itself, no dock could be imagined more adapted for a small craft like ours. We immediately set to work and landed our goods and leaving our men to prepare our suppers took a stroll up country.

Frederick Weld, wearing stout leather boots, moleskin trousers, a heavy serge shirt and a wide-brimmed hat, spent the next three days exploring the hinterland in the area of today's Ward. With a firearm slung over his shoulder, the tall, reed-slim young Englishman was in his element.

Weld Cone from Ward Beach. Seabirds line the Flaxbourne River.

The lower reaches of the Flaxbourne River.

Weld found all that Workman promised and a great deal more. Between the coast and the northern end of the Kaikoura Range, in an area Weld considered was about "some thirty miles by ten or twelve" (50 kilometres by 16 or 20 kilometres), was everything that he and his partner required to establish a sheep station on a grand scale. Whichever way he happened to look the hills rolled and dipped and were covered with tall tussocks that swayed in the soft wind. Weld, moved by what he saw, put pen to paper and described "a magnificent expanse of undulating grass lands made beautiful by the deep shades and curling mists of morning".

Between the low hills well-sheltered gullies and hollows provided a habitat for cabbage trees, flax and toetoe. Streams were abundant; and, most significantly, there was a safe harbour close to a suitable site for a homestead.

On 27 September Weld, Caverhill and Wade travelled north, taking with them provisions and blankets:

We followed the river as far as open country when we turned to the right and passing a lake some two miles [3 kilometres] in length [Lake Elterwater] traversed a plain and its hillocks and after three hours walking stood on a low range of grass hills with the Cape Campbell hills on our right and Kaiparatehau lagoon [Lake Grassmere], a sheet of water much resembling the Wairarapa lower lake, stretched out before us.

As we descended to its banks we surprised a great quantity of ducks on the low lands that immediately surround it and I shot several while the others endeavoured to boil our camp kettle by means of docks and toe-toe stalks as not a vestige of wood was to be seen . . .

140

Leaving Kaiparatehau behind us, from the next ridge we saw a brook which we thought to be bushed but when we reached it at nightfall the timber was found to consist of nothing but a few miserable manuka shrubs. Just before encamping we saw two large wild dogs beating like setters for quail and by means of skilful creeping and covering behind my hat I managed to knock over one of them with ball as he came up to and bounded past me.

We made ourselves comfortable for the night with the ducks I had shot but could not get enough wood for a good fire and neither I nor my companions could sleep for cold.

On the night of 30 September the *Fidele* nosed out of the mouth of the Flaxbourne River, and in the evening of the following day, right on dusk, the cutter passed Wellington Heads.

Until it was properly roaded, the Rimutaka Range made travel between Wellington and the Wairarapa more than difficult.

Blind River to the East Coast around Cape Campbell to Kekerengu", perhaps as much as 80,000 hectares, they would pay £12 per annum.

They would name their new station Flaxbourne.

Convinced by now that his future lay in New Zealand, Charles Clifford had sent to England for his fiancée to join him. Marianne was the vivacious daughter of John Hercy of Critchfield House in Berkshire, and she brought with her £8000 and an entourage of servants. She expected much of her servants and was intolerant of their failings. In a letter to a friend in England she wrote: "All cooks have tempers and she has a sulky one and moreover does not speak the truth . . . I got rid of that Irish woman who turned out such a character . . . it is very odd that we cannot get men or women who will behave with us."

Charles Clifford and Marianne were married on 13 January 1847 in Wellington. The first of their four children, George, was born in October in that same year. In the late summer of 1847 Charles and Marianne Clifford went to Sydney, where Charles set about purchasing the very best Merino ewes he could find (they would bring down the stud Merino rams from Wharekaka later in the year).

The land that Clifford and Weld wanted belonged by right of conquest to Ngati Toa. The chief of that tribe was Te Puaha (successor to Te Rauparaha), whose pa was at Porirua. Charles Clifford and Tom Caverhill set out for Porirua, where they found the chief in an agreeable frame of mind. He had no objections to granting Clifford and his absent partner the exclusive right to run sheep on Ngati Toa land across the water. A lease was drawn up, and for "all of the land from the

Meantime, Weld was busy with two projects: the building of a prefabricated homestead designed by Tom Caverhill that would be dismantled and shipped to

Flaxbourne, and the construction of the *Petrel*, a small cutter of 9 tonnes that would provide a vital link with Wellington.

Four steamships were chartered to bring the sheep and other livestock – including five horses and a mule – from Australia to New Zealand. A large but unrecorded number of sheep apparently died during the voyage. The partners intended to unload their sheep near Cape Campbell and drive them to the homestead site, a comparatively simple task. But it was not to be. A long spell of rough winter weather forced the vessels to run for cover in Port Underwood (south-east of present-day Picton), and a shortage of feed meant that the sheep had to be put ashore.

The overland trip from Port Underwood to the new station, overseen by Weld and Clifford, was both difficult and tedious. There was incessant rain and hail to contend with; rivers ran high and caused frustrating delays; tracks had to be cut to allow the sheep to get through bush and scrub; and wild dogs were troublesome. Nineteen days passed before men and stock came to the Awatere River, 25 kilometres from their new home. By now they were out of basic supplies and, because Clifford had broken Weld's gun, they were unable to hunt. They made do on wild cabbage and mutton.

But at last the sheep – about 2500 – were grazing contentedly on the grassy hills around the narrow lower valley of the Flaxbourne River. Soon after, the *Petrel* made her initial voyage to the station and two weeks later Weld was pleased to note that the homestead, to be named Grassmere, was nearly finished.

The building, painted white with a shingle roof, was located on the true right of the Flaxbourne River about

Droving Merinos.

142

a kilometre from the sea, thus allowing access for small boats such as the *Petrel*. As Weld commented, "I shall be able to have any comfort I require brought almost to my door."

Marianne Clifford missed England very much and talked longingly of seeing her family again. It would appear that Marianne's dreadful homesickness, and her husband's business ventures, were the main reasons they returned to England in April 1848.

The following December, while the Cliffords were still in England, Weld and Caverhill went on business to Wharekaka. There it was that Tom Caverhill drowned in the Ruamahunga River. Caverhill, a top horseman in any company, was working cattle across the river, which was up a bit, dirty and running swift. He put the cattle across without difficulty, but the leading beasts, once out of the water, started to go in the wrong direction. To head them off, Caverhill went downstream a bit to cross the river. But the far bank was much steeper than he had expected and as the horse struggled to climb the bank, disaster struck: Caverhill's mount lost its footing and fell backwards. Before the horrified eyes of several stockmen both horse and rider were swept into a deep hole under the bank. Caverhill's body would not be recovered until the following day.

The death of Tom Caverhill shattered Frederick Weld. In later life he would often refer to the gritty Scotsman with deep affection. Caverhill had been there when it counted: it was he who had made Wharekaka what it was, and he who had taught Weld so much about sheep and station life. When a saddened Weld returned to Flaxbourne it was impossible for him not to reflect on how Caverhill had designed and helped to build the very home he lived in and had so much come to love. Tom Caverhill could not be replaced.

The not unexpected arrival in the district of other well-bred sheepraisers, while agreeable inasmuch as it provided Weld with more stimulating company than could be found among his staff, had a serious down side. The clamour for land was great, growing louder by the week, and Clifford and Weld's hold on the obviously oversized Flaxbourne was tenuous at best.

When in March 1847 Governor Grey had negotiated the Wairau Purchase with Ngati Toa, Te Puaha had failed to mention the fact that Clifford and Weld held a lease on a large piece of the land he was selling. Te Puaha's silence on this point may well have had something to do with the £3000 his tribe received under the deal.

The New Zealand Company took over control of the land and in 1848 brought in a new act that required all "squatters" in the Nelson district – including Clifford and Weld – to apply for a depasturing licence, giving details of area, boundaries, stock numbers, and so on. As a result of this Flaxbourne, which even Clifford and Weld admitted was too big to run properly, was reduced to 32,000 hectares. No matter: Flaxbourne was still an empire of grass where a man's dreams were limited only by his imagination.

The Flaxbourne flock had by 1850 increased to 11,000; six shepherds were on the payroll. Such was the quality of their stud rams that they sold for £20 apiece, the highest price in the country. It is worth noting that in 1855 the pastoral licence fee for the station came to £25. On top of this they were charged £66 on the basis of the stock they carried. So for less than £100 a year, the price of four of their stud rams, they had control of 32,000 hectares of some of the very best sheep country in New Zealand.

Where the river enters the sea.

SIXTEEN

A NEW RUN

When the Cliffords returned to Flaxbourne from England in November 1850, Charles's younger brother, 20-year-old Alphonso, was with them. It was his intention to eventually take up land in New Zealand. He had with him £1000, a tidy sum with which to bring ambition to fruition. But first he had to learn the ropes.

With their sheep doing wonderfully well on Flaxbourne, the partners were keen to wind down Wharekaka. Not only had Weld come to loathe the mosquito-ridden place but, since the death of Tom Caverhill, it was upsetting to go there. He would never forget Christmas Eve 1848, when they had cleaned up Caverhill's body ready to be shipped to Wellington, or

Christmas and Boxing Day, when he had accompanied Caverhill's widow and children to Wellington.

The month after the Cliffords returned to New Zealand the main body of the Canterbury Association's colonists reached Lyttelton in four ships. With the opening up of much of the interior for sheep runs imminent, Clifford and Weld resolved to establish a second station in the South Island.

From about 1847 onwards coastal traffic – schooners and cutters – had been a common sight off the east coast of the South Island as they worked back and forth between Wellington and Lyttelton. Perhaps

The Kaikoura Range.

146

the first regular steamer on this stretch of coastline was the Government survey ship, HMS *Acheron*. In late April 1849 the officers and men of the *Acheron* had been invited ashore for a few days' relaxation at Flaxbourne station.

Weld had learnt that a party of men from the Acheron had earlier in the month gone ashore south of the Hurunui River, close to the northern boundary of the Canterbury Block. They had called in at Motunau station, which had been "taken" by Joseph Greenwood three years previously. A large expanse of land north of Motunau, running from there to the Hurunui River and beyond, had, Clifford and Weld discovered, not yet been taken up.

Frederick Weld had determined to explore this potential site for a sheep station himself, so when the *Acheron*, called in at Flaxbourne on the way to Lyttelton in late November 1850, Weld became a passenger. On 4 December he started back to Flaxbourne on foot. Travelling with him was noted bushman Charles Wilkinson.

Soon they came to the 24,000-hectare Motunau station. Beyond lay the lower reaches of the Hurunui River country. This, Weld soon realised, was the perfect place to establish a sheep station. It was right on the coast and the country was not unlike that of Flaxbourne. Moreover, it was no great distance – and easy travelling at that – from the port of Lyttelton. Also, with the arrival of large numbers of settlers in Christchurch, a new local market for livestock and fresh meat would be created.

As Weld continued north he surveyed the options for overlanding sheep from Flaxbourne to their new run – providing, of course, that it was not taken up in the meantime. In late 1850 no practical route had been

The Clarence River above its confluence with the Acheron.

found linking the Nelson district and the Canterbury Plains. He arrived back at Flaxbourne 12 or 13 days after leaving Lyttelton.

On 20 December 1850, in quest of a practicable stock route, he headed up the Awatere River. With him was Flaxbourne's newest hired hand – English-born 19-year-old George Lovegrove, just five weeks in New Zealand. In the vicinity of today's Upcot station they travelled through a narrow gorge; later they crossed what would one day become the biggest station in the land – Molesworth station. At last the river dwindled to a "mere brook" and they found the pass a party of Maoris had spoken of, through which they could without difficulty reach North Canterbury. They named the 1040-metre saddle Barefell Pass and spent a "cold, wet, and thoroughly cheerless" Christmas Eve there.

Weld considered it impossible to take stock along certain stretches of the coast between Flaxbourne and Canterbury. He was proven wrong.

Beyond the pass a stream flowed south and south-west; Weld, somewhat ambitiously, named it the Guide River. Presently the Guide flowed into a bigger river that Weld was certain was the Clarence. It was in fact the Acheron, named after the vessel.

With the already poor weather deteriorating, and supplies running low, Weld and Lovegrove topped a high point, the better to judge their position. Weld's mistake in identifying the Acheron was only the start of his errors. His real problem was that he was far to the north of where he presumed himself to be – the low country around Hanmer Springs. Looking to the south-east, he believed a stream flowing towards distant "cloud-mantled hills" to be the Leader, which flowed into the Waiau and which he had forded north of the Hurunui only weeks previously. The river was in truth the Dillon, another tributary of the Clarence River.

Weld was certain he had discovered a practical stock route and, seeing no reason to go further, the pair retraced their steps to Flaxbourne. While Weld was searching for a stock route, his partner hadn't wasted any time. On Boxing Day he had applied for (and was duly granted) a licence to depasture stock on a roughly triangular 23,500-hectare block running up the Hurunui River from the sea to a point 8 kilometres below its junction with the Pahau River.

On 20 January 1851 Frederick Weld left Flaxbourne for a lengthy trip to England, so the task of establishing the new run would not be his. A month later Charles Clifford put 720 wethers on the road. It was not his intention to stock the new run with these sheep: they would be sold as mutton to the new Canterbury settlers, who, by all accounts, were starved of fresh meat.

The droving team – Alphonso Clifford, George Lovegrove and two ex-whalers – could have hardly been less experienced. Alphonso carried Weld's rather hastily drawn map, but with Lovegrove's first-hand knowledge to rely on he would have little use for it at first. The journey was tough on man and beast. In places the Awatere valley was choked with scrub – tangled forests of matagouri, higher than a tall man and armed with sharp barbs, hillfaces covered with the aptly named speargrass. Soon the sheep were footsore; they had on occasion to be manhandled across the river. It was brutal, back-breaking work. Despite 12-hour days, progress was painfully slow.

When they reached Barefell Pass they had been going for 11 days. Alphonso Clifford was worried sick: they had not planned for the trip to take this long, and already provisions were low. Down the Guide River they went, until they reached the river Weld had thought was the Clarence. By this time Lovegrove's understanding of what lay ahead was no clearer than young Alphonso's. They crossed the river, drove the sheep up and over a saddle, and went down what they thought was the Leader (almost certainly the present-day Leader Dale, a different river altogether). Eventually they came to the real Clarence River.

If Weld's map had been confusing before, now it was doubly so. They forded the Clarence and climbed the hills on its true right. Ahead lay inhospitable terrain. In fact, rough country stared them in the face no matter which way they cared to look. Worse, the sheep, barely able to hobble along, were just about done for. Hungry, weary and totally despondent, the drovers simply left the sheep where they were and returned to Flaxbourne.

"Weld has made a great mistake in supposing he has found a practicable route," Clifford commented, "he was misled by a mirage or something else because it is impossible he could have been within 30 miles [50 kilometres] as far south as he supposed himself to be." In due course Frederick Weld would receive a letter from his partner telling him of their mutual loss. A pithy and rather cutting extract read: "But then the Kaikouras are so barbarous, and everyone about so stupid, and your maps, my dear Weld, so inaccurate."

While Weld was in England he found himself something of a celebrity and was frequently asked what it was like being a sheep farmer in faraway New Zealand. Finally Weld put pen to paper and he wrote a pamphlet entitled *Hints to Intending Sheep Farmers in New Zealand*. It raced through four editions and for some time was regarded as a "must" for anyone contemplating such an occupation.

In early 1852 Alphonso Clifford was again put in charge of a droving party. The purpose was to stock the new station, Stonyhurst, with 1500 ewes and lambs. This time they would take the sheep via the coastline. With all their supplies in a whaleboat that could be beckoned ashore, they headed south along the heavy sands of the coast. They reached their destination with the loss of only one sheep.

Before long Alphonso Clifford became a runholder in his own right when he took up Waikakahi station, the southernmost of the early Canterbury runs, in November 1853. In the following year Charles Clifford and Frederick Weld were both elected to the first General Assembly: Clifford was the first speaker in the House of Representatives, while Weld represented the Wairau electorate.

Stock continued to be overlanded via the Awatere River, Barefell Pass, then a newly discovered route over Jollies Pass, but droving contractors considered it too long. The Provincial Government approached Frederick Weld with a view to finding a quicker way from Nelson to Canterbury. Weld accepted gladly, perhaps recognising a golden opportunity to redeem himself after the earlier fiasco. In the meantime, Alphonso Clifford had disposed of his station and, at a loose end before returning to England, was only too pleased to accept Weld's invitation to accompany him.

In late March 1855, travelling light, Weld and Clifford reached the wild, forested country of the upper Wairau River. The upper Wairau was believed to be impassable as a stock route, but Weld and Clifford came to a fair-sized river, flowing from the west, that merged with the Wairau. Weld in his report would call this the West Wairau (later the Rainbow).

They climbed a ridge to the south, and from the highest point of the ridge, Mount Weld (2118 metres), they beheld a wondrous sight:

Light mists floating about the summit slightly impeded our view, yet did not from an altitude of nearly 7,000 feet [2140 metres] above sea level, prevent us from ascertaining that the inland grass country lay below us. At our feet, to the southeast, lay a valley dotted with miniature lakes or pools; beyond and around it, grassy and bare-topped hills and narrow valleys. In the distance, bearing about east, we made out the landward Kaikouras amongst the clouds and mist, with the Barefell Pass. Immediately on our left, the southeast branch of the Wairau flowed out of a rock-bound gorge, whilst to our right little was visible but craggy and snow-patched mountains, in which the valley of the west Wairau seemed soon to break and lose itself.

Frederick Weld and Alphonso Clifford became the first Europeans to explore the Tarndale Flats: "The most remarkable feature of Tarndale is undoubtedly the

The Clifford party came by this coastline in 1852 with their sheep.

little lakes, or 'tarns', from which I derived its name. They are six or seven in number, not all visible at once, but lie scattered amongst low undulations of land, at the north end of the valley."

Weld had made plans to pick up supplies and fresh horses in the Acheron valley. His specific orders to Knight and McCade were to "keep a good fire going" – this, of course, would help him to pinpoint the exact location. A day after leaving Tarndale Weld and Clifford spotted campfire smoke and made haste to link up with the men. Following an overnight camp at the junction of the Acheron and Clarence, Clifford and Knight set off for Flaxbourne, but Weld still had much to do.

Taking McCade with him, he headed up the Clarence and established a depot at the junction of Jollies Pass stream. He discovered a saddle between the headwaters of the Clarence and the upper reaches of the Wairau; this would become known as Island Saddle. Burning the country as he went, Weld made his way to Stonyhurst station.

Weld had opened up two new routes to North Canterbury: "That by the Clarence is the shorter by about five miles [8 kilometres] and the river is easier to ford; whilst the route by the Acheron is the most perfect level, less stony, and at present has the advantage of having been, for the greater part, cleared by successive fires."

The Nelson Provincial Government was well satisfied with Weld's achievement. Weld's route – Tophouse to Tarndale and then down the Acheron to the Clarence – cut about 200 kilometres off the previous journey, and the trip from Nelson to Canterbury was reduced to about six days. The route

Weld's stock route of 1855, linking Nelson and Canterbury, followed the course of the Wairau River.

was to prove popular: in 1863 a total of 61,420 sheep would arrive in Canterbury – 12,520 by sea; 10,850 overlanded from Otago; and a staggering 38,050 put ashore at Nelson and taken by drovers by Frederick Weld's stock route of 1855.

In 1859 Weld, on another return trip to England, married Filumena, whose mother Laura was a member of the Clifford family. Filumena and Frederick would have 13 children, of which 12 survived infancy. Also in 1859 Charles Clifford received a baronetcy (for his services to New Zealand). He retired from politics a year later and returned to England, although he made a number of visits to New Zealand. His partnership with Weld continued as before.

From about 1863 the Welds lived at Brackenfield, a small estate roughly midway between Stonyhurst and Christchurch. Although generally disillusioned with politics, the idealistic Weld, by now Native Minister, was the man Governor Grey turned to when other political leaders refused to accept vice-regal authority over Maori land confiscation. At Grey's request Weld formed a government in 1864; he was Premier of New Zealand until the following year when, having been defeated on a vote in the House, he resigned.

In 1869 Charles Clifford approached Weld with a view to bringing his son George into their partnership. Weld was not in favour of this and Clifford offered to buy him out. Weld was prepared to sell his share in Stonyhurst, but they could not agree on a price and the partnership continued as before.

Weld and his family spent some time in England before Weld became the Governor of Western Australia in 1871. Two years later he relinquished his interest in Stonyhurst to Clifford and George Clifford took over the running of both stations with, of course, managers on each of them. Weld's term of office in Western Australia came to an end in 1875. He became Governor

of Tasmania before moving on to become Governor of the British Protectorate of Malaya. In 1882 he was knighted and five years later he returned to England.

Sir Frederick Weld died at his family home in 1891 at the age of 68. Sir Charles Clifford died in England two years later at 78. Together they had started the first sheep station in the country, Wharekaka, and had established the first great sheep station in the South Island, Flaxbourne. Arguably the two Englishmen were the most significant of the early colonial pastoralists.

At the time of Charles Clifford's death the manager on Flaxbourne was Henry Vavasour, son of William Vavasour, the man who had been involved in the very early part of the Wharekaka story. Born in England in 1850, Henry Vavasour was one of four sons, all of whom had been quite fascinated by their father's stories of life in faraway New Zealand.

For some years after his return to England in 1844 (to marry Mary Clifford) William Vavasour, especially after a visit home by either Charles Clifford or Frederick Weld, talked of returning to New Zealand, but his general health was poor and he died in 1869. Young Henry, inspired by Clifford's and Weld's thrilling tales of life in the South Island, longed to go there for himself.

When Henry Vavasour at last arrived in New Zealand he was just 21, his education not long finished. His first call was at Flaxbourne, the station of his dead father's cousins. He remained there for three or four years and became very accomplished in station life. Following a number of business ventures, none of which were especially successful, he returned to Flaxbourne as manager in 1884.

Frederick's son, Everade Weld, born in England in 1868, had also dreamed that one day he would become a sheep farmer in New Zealand. So it was that, some 44 years after his father had first come ashore near the mouth of the lovely Flaxbourne River, Everade Weld

The Inland Kaikoura Range from the upper Awatere Valley, in the vicinity of Barefell Pass. Steve Satterthwaite, on the Muller station, pushes his cattle along in the direction of Barefell Pass.

arrived at the station to work under Henry Vavasour. He found everything he aspired to, the kind of lifestyle impossible to find at home. Truly New Zealand was all and everything his father had claimed it to be.

Everade Weld's arrival at Flaxbourne coincided with a plague of rabbits on the place. As one observer noted, "if one went on to the station and shouted, a very wave of rabbits would roll over the hills reminding one of a swell at sea".

By the early 1890s over 160 kilometres of rabbit-proof fencing had been erected, but even that was not completely effective. Once, having just about eaten out a fenced-off area, the rabbits turned their attentions to a cabbage tree. When they had eaten most of the way through it, the tree collapsed and fell across a fence,

forming a bridge over which the rabbits swarmed to a clean block of land.

At any one time between 40 and 80 men might be employed to deal with the rabbits; one year, when even more were hired on a contract basis, there were over 100 men on the station working solely on eradicating the creatures. The rabbits were hunted with teams of dogs and warrens were dug out.

Between 1 April 1893 and 31 March 1894 over 500,000 top-grade rabbit skins were exported from Flaxbourne; the total number of rabbits killed far exceeded this figure. But still no real impact on their overall numbers was made: rabbits were as plentiful as raindrops in the wet season. As a result, the woolclip, which in 1893 was 741 bales, fell to half what it had been a few years previously.

In 1894 Everade Weld was put in charge of rabbit extermination operations on Flaxbourne. Rabbit poisons had proved largely unreliable and had not even been tried on Flaxbourne, but when a new poison came on the market, phosphorised pollard, Weld believed that this might be the solution. He dispensed with traps, saying they were "as good as useless". When all of the traps from the station were collected up they made, it was said, "a pile as large as a four-roomed house".

Weld was right about the new poison, and soon there was an obvious drop in rabbit numbers. The introduction of phosphorised pollard, however, was also the final nail in the coffin for the station's wekas, which were already hounded by introduced predators, including ferrets, weasels and cats.

Henry Vavasour's time as manager on Flaxbourne came to an end in 1897, when he purchased nearby Ugbrooke station from his cousin William Clifford. The Cliffords offered the position to the man who was doing such a magnificent job of cleaning up the rabbits, Everade Weld. Indeed, just two years later the battle had been decisively won and the woolclip was a healthy 1500 bales. The Cliffords were immensely grateful for the part Weld had played, for between 1892 and 1896 the station had run at a loss and they'd had to come up with an extra £16,000 to keep it afloat.

The turn of the century saw a major reduction in the size of Flaxbourne when the Cliffords decided to sell 3800 hectares from the Woodside run, at the southern end of the station. Now Flaxbourne stood at a compact 24,000 hectares. With the rabbits finally beaten (although five rabbiters were kept on the payroll) and wool prices climbing steadily, the future for the Cliffords looked as bright as a spring day in Marlborough.

But thunderclouds were gathering. For several years the Government had been casting a predatory eye on Flaxbourne: with its easy rolling hill country, plus the fact that the railway would soon run right through it, the property was ideal for closer settlement. As far back as 1898 they had approached the Cliffords with a view to purchasing Flaxbourne. Again in 1902 they asked the question: Flaxbourne would never be sold, was the answer.

The Government was not to be thwarted – they passed the Land for Settlement Act, which gave the Crown the right to take over any run it wanted. So it was that in February 1903 the Government spelled it out to the Cliffords: they intended to take Flaxbourne. The days of the first great sheep station in the South Island were numbered.

In the months that followed lawyers and land valuers for both parties could not reach an agreement, and the Cliffords turned to the Compensation Court. The case opened in the Blenheim Courthouse on 11 December 1903, and the most important land law case held in the country to that date also turned out to be the longest. After two years the final judgment was issued: the Cliffords were to be paid £181,000 for Flaxbourne, considerably less than the £410,000 they had asked for. Weary of the whole sorry business, the Cliffords agreed to the Court's decision, provided they could retain 5000 hectares in the Cape Campbell region. The Government's lawyers agreed.

The subdivision of Flaxbourne, known as the Flaxbourne Settlement, was held by ballot in July and August 1905; in addition, a number of small sections were taken up near what became the Ward township. The two main ballots were for small grazing runs, none over 1200 hectares, to farm-sized properties. The sections at Ward were between 2 and 10 hectares in size. Flaxbourne was broken up into 107 separate land holdings.

SEVENTEEN

BOTH PAST AND PRESENT

The Canterbury dawning was altogether beautiful. A warm easterly airflow drifted in from the nearby coast as the first rays of the sun speared across the rural landscape and cast a magical glow upon the small and graceful church. This was the Roman Catholic Church of the Most Holy Passion, at the southern end of Amberley. Although it was about 130 years old, it had stood here only since the mid-1950s.

For several years after 1863 Frederick Weld and his family had lived close to Amberley at Brackenfield, but he had actually bought the 300-hectare block of land in July 1861, when no settlement had existed in the area.

Late in 1861 Weld had designed a "very commodious and nice-looking house", a 16-room dwelling of kauri and black pine. The house stood on a commanding site, the driveway flanked by regiments of exotic trees. Shrubberies and flower gardens were established, and to the park-like environment Weld introduced deer and gamebirds from England. Brackenfield estate was a place fit for a country gentleman.

Weld's ambitions for Brackenfield did not end there. He envisaged the estate as the hub of a thriving township – and all indications were that the forthcoming railway would pass very close to

Weld's church at Amberley.

Looking across the Hurunui River in the late evening to high country which was a part of the original Stonyhurst run.

Brackenfield. Weld, somewhat impetuously, went to the point of having the site surveyed. The town, to be called Brackenridge, would need a church and Weld was quite prepared to finance such a place himself. He did not intend the church to be a family monument, rather a physical expression of the faith that would sustain him for all the days of his life.

Weld had a great deal to do with the design, construction and finishing of the church. In a time when craftsmen prided themselves on their painstaking attention to detail, almost all of the joints in the building were lovingly dovetailed – hardly a nail was used. Stained-glass windows were made to order by a London firm. This church ranked among the oldest Catholic churches in Canterbury, predated only by the one at Akaroa.

But by the time the church was finished the planned railway line, to Weld's dismay, had been rerouted much closer to the coast than he had been given to understand, through today's Amberley; his hopes for a Brackenridge had been defeated. The church, with seating for 150, was left without a congregation until it was moved to its present site in 1954–55. The Brackenfield house was demolished in 1964.

The first homestead or manager's dwelling on the station.

For me, so many years later, the church provided a tangible link to the story of the first great sheep station in the South Island. It was still half in sun, half in shadow, when I headed north out of Amberley.

Despite being early April, it felt as warm as spring by the time I came to the Greta valley, and the gentle breeze of the dawn had become a powerful force. There had been a long run of hot, dry weather in North Canterbury and many station people had had no option but to sustain their animals with feed stockpiled for the winter. That was going to be bad news if the winter turned out to be as bad as 1992.

But chilly days, and even colder nights, seemed a long way away as I picked out a signpost to Stonyhurst – and followed it. Now, on a back road, it was impossible for me not to think of another autumn day long ago when Frederick Weld, having discovered two new stock routes between Nelson and Canterbury, continued his journey to Stonyhurst with McCade.

The first manager on Stonyhurst station was William Hyde Harris, who was already on the place when Alphonso Clifford came down the coast with sheep.

159

Hyde Harris was considered a great horseman in a time when that accolade counted for much. He could, however, be rather reckless. One day he went down hard with his horse on top of him. He was pronounced dead, taken back to the homestead and stretched out on a bed to await funeral arrangements. Overnight, however, he made a miraculous recovery and by breakfast time he was as right as rain. The place where he fell became known as Harris's Fall.

With Alphonso Clifford spending a great deal of time on the new run, he and Hyde Harris soon became very good friends. In November 1853 Hyde Harris took up a run on the Waitaki next to Alphonso Clifford's, both runs being a part of the original Waikakahi block. Hyde Harris remained there much longer than Clifford did, but in 1866 he would return to manage both Stonyhurst and Flaxbourne.

In late 1853 George Lovegrove took over from Hyde Harris on Stonyhurst. He stayed for three years before taking up the same position on Flaxbourne, where he remained until 1871, making him the longest serving manager on the first great sheep station in the South Island.

Following Lovegrove on Stonyhurst came Robert Boys. His favourite trick, performed time after time, was to place a shilling on the tip of his boot, then shoot it off with a pistol. Boys would perform this party piece time after time without managing to shoot himself in the foot.

In 1863 Clifford and Weld decided to sell off the part of Stonyhurst beyond the Waikari River to the west. The Greta block, 10,000 hectares of mostly scrubby wilderness ranged by wild cattle of mean disposition and wild pigs by the score, was taken on by

Peter and Fiona Douglas-Clifford's home. The Happy Valley and Motunau station country lie beyond.

John and Michael Studholm and Thomas Sanderson. They called it Greta Peaks.

Wild pigs were also a problem on Stonyhurst. In 1878 a shepherd, P. Goldin, was offered an eight-month contract to kill as many as he could. Goldin tackled his task with an enthusiasm matched only, one suspects, by that of his dogs. At the end of eight months he had been paid for 1202 pig snouts; in the following year his tally was even better – 1322.

At the time of the Flaxbourne subdivision in 1905 George Clifford sold off a further 5000 hectares of Stonyhurst to avoid increased land taxes. However, the sale of Flaxbourne left him with capital to spare and, as well as indulging himself in his passion for racehorses, he invested heavily in the Canterbury Frozen Meat Company.

When his father George died in 1930 Charles Clifford, the only son, inherited Stonyhurst. He would become the first Clifford to be truly classed as an owner/manager; his father, with his business and racing interests, had mostly resided at Riccarton. Charles Clifford, who did not marry, died in 1938. It was his nephew John Douglas-Clifford to whom the station was handed down in 1948.

On a bright and sunny autumn day – almost 50 years after 24-year-old John Douglas-Clifford had taken control of Stonyhurst – the man himself was showing me around the old, rundown homestead tucked away in a stand of exotic trees. This was the first substantial homestead built on the place and dated to the 1850s. I counted five bedrooms, a kitchen, a pocket-sized office and a sitting room dominated by a huge fireplace. The house was in a neglected condition but not beyond repair.

Earlier we had driven around most of the now 1600-hectare station. It was good country, easy country, perhaps the best part of the original run. There was a narrow coastal belt then low hills; the wind was seldom absent. John Douglas-Clifford, who had more or less retired 10 years earlier, had explained that the station was now held in three separate titles, one for each of his sons. The station was still run as one, however, and John and Peter, the older of the sons, had that responsibility. John and his Australian wife Robin lived in the renovated cookshop complex; in time they hoped to reclaim the grand old homestead. Peter and his Scottish wife Fiona lived in a lovely home on the clifftops overlooking the sea.

They ran the same halfbred flock that George Clifford had run well over a century earlier, and they would winter 15,000 ewes. The men were working with cattle when I had arrived at the station; the Herefords numbered upwards of 2000. In 1925 there had been 30 men on the payroll; today they employed three – two shepherds and a tractor driver.

I stood in the sitting room of the old homestead with its cob partitions, thick, well-insulated, and its ceiling low enough to bother a very tall man. On a cold winter's night this would have been a snug room in which to sit by the fire and mull over the forthcoming day's work, a glass of brandy in hand, the occasional cigar to draw on.

From an adjoining room John Douglas-Clifford spoke. I did not catch what he said and went to find him. He was poking a dead possum with the toe of his boot.

"That looks good, doesn't it?" he said, picked it up rather delicately by a curled, stiffened tail and turfed it outside into the tall grass. "That's better," he said, rubbing the palms of his hands on his trouser legs.

The present-day homestead on the station.

EIGHTEEN

FLAXBOURNE NO MORE

It was raining. It was cold. The most recent weather forecast I'd picked up didn't promise any improvement – not for a few days, anyway. I was wearing a beat-up Driza-Bone with the collar turned up; my moleskins showed why off-white was not a sensible colour in my line of work; the cleats of my boots were caked with dried mud. I'd needed a shave yesterday, a haircut a week before that. As I knocked on the front door of the homestead at Wharanui station I might have resembled an old-time swagger after a handout.

I was greeted affably by Lecester Murray and his American wife Laura. After handshakes I said apologetically, "Please forgive my rough appearance, I've been on the road –"

Lecester made a sharp cutting motion with the flat of his hand: apologies weren't needed. Lecester was also attired in work clothing, although the big difference was that his were clean.

"You look like you could use a cup of tea," he said with his genuine smile of welcome still fixed firmly in place.

He was not wrong about that: I had made a late crossing of Cook Strait, reached Blenheim in the wee small hours then slept in the back of my vehicle, comfortable in my Aussie swag.

Slipping off my boots, I said, "You'll be pleased about the rain, I expect?" Discussion of the weather was not small talk in the country, it was right up there with the latest info on the All Blacks.

Twenty-eight-year-old Lecester Murray was very pleased about the rain. I had no doubt that other station people along Marlborough's east coast, and into North Canterbury for that matter, would be rejoicing about the wet stuff, too. Up north, however, it was another story altogether.

We sat down around a big table. The Murrays had just finished a meal.

"There's plenty over," Laura said. "Would you like some?"

Maybe I did look like a road-weary swagger on the make, after all.

I asked about the yellow flag hanging at half mast on the approach to the homestead. Limp and bedraggled, and not all of a proud flutter, it wasn't the sort of flag you'd willingly run behind in battle.

Lecester let his wife reply. "It's the flag of New Mexico."

I gathered that her home state was New Mexico, the place where Billy the Kid was gunned down by Sheriff Pat Garrett.

"Always fancied a trip there, y'know," I said. "Must be really something."

"It's great!" Lecester said. He had been there several times to visit Laura's folks. With his smooth good looks, easy manner and clipped, almost English accent, Lecester Murray would have gone down a real treat.

When the Cliffords sold the Woodside run in 1901 Charles Frank Murray had taken up the part that became Wharanui. Murray, his wife Jessie and their two children came from North Canterbury. Wharanui stood at 2500 hectares and, apart from the few buildings that made up an out-station, it was pretty much virgin

Wharanui homestead.

Corriedales awaiting shearing on Wharanui.

country. The land was clad with heavy timber, rampant ferns on the lower hills and flats, and tussock running out to the sandhills along the coastline. A man could make his own mark on country like that.

It didn't take much to make a start – just a box of matches. The firing of the land was not done without careful thought. Stock required shelter if they were to remain contented, and good stock were as good as gold, cash in the bank. Murray left many stands of trees to provide shelter for his near 1000-strong herd of cattle, mostly Shorthorns. The beasts, however, rampaged through the tussock and fern and, over a prolonged period, the constant trampling and overgrazing practically destroyed it.

Within a dozen years Murray and his workforce of seven or eight men (labour was readily available and cheap to boot) had, by planting English grasses, dramatically altered the face of Wharanui. Out on his now cultivated hills Murray ran 7000 well-contented crossbred sheep, the usual Merino ewe/English Leicester ram parenthood. His English Leicester stud had 250 breeding ewes. At shearing time the average weight of each fleece was 3.6 kilograms; the woolclip was sent direct to London. Stock fattened for the marketplace was normally taken to the freezing works at Picton.

Murray added two fine young Hereford bulls to his Shorthorn cattle; a herd of dairy cattle also grazed on the flatlands near the coast. That had started with the purchase of five in-calf Shorthorn heifers from the stud at Gungaggi, in New South Wales.

Lecester ushered me into a huge billiards room. The mounted heads of game animals gazed down from the wood-panelled walls; one Murray at least had been a trophy hunter. Lecester indicated a small, alcove: "My office." The space contained a small fireplace, a big, rather cluttered desk, and a good working atmosphere.

"I could cheerfully kill for an office like this," I pointed out.

Lecester Murray chuckled. Charles Murray had, he explained, started to build this homestead shortly after he had arrived, but it wasn't finished until about 1918. Today it appeared much as it was at the end of the First World War: two-storeyed, 21 rooms, wood-panelled walls of what appeared to be cedar and polished floors of what was undoubtedly matai. All up it was about 700 square metres of gracious living space. Looking around this marvellous old home, which had never been owned by anyone outside the Murray family, I thought what a great place it must have been to grow up in.

Like so many other stations, Wharanui had been gradually whittled down in size, the last significant subdivision occurring when Lecester's father and uncle had divided it between them. Now the Wharanui homestead block stood at just 700 hectares – farm-sized, really.

Outside it was still raining, though not as heavily as before. Still cold, but.

Lecester was keen to get back to work, and I went with him. Corriedales bleated in the yards: they ran 4000 of them on the place, as well as some Hereford cattle. The woolshed that stood nearby had been built by Charles Murray in the early 1890s.

Across the road from the homestead stood St Oswald's Anglican Church, built in 1927 by Charles Murray as a memorial to his son Hector, who had died of tuberculosis. Today, Lecester told me, all denominations used the church.

Beyond the homestead the hills were brown and

St Oswald's Anglican Church, Wharanui.

undernourished looking; it would take more rain that this to change it. Mist covered much of those hills, and I felt I might just as well have been in the Scottish Highlands. It would take a return trip to get some decent photographs.

On a wet July day I visited the valley of the Flaxbourne and followed that winding river to where it flowed into the sea. On a grassy flat beside the tranquil river, below low hills, exotic trees roughly marked the site of Frederick Weld's homestead, Grassmere. Nothing remained of the house itself or, for that matter, of the other buildings that once stood here.

It was like looking at hallowed ground. This was where the first great sheep station in the South Island had really started. This place had had a profound influence on my life: without Flaxbourne – and the stations that followed – there would have been no Station Country books for me to work on.

I did not have to drive too far to reach the coast. Driftwood was piled high on a bleak-looking Ward Beach; seabirds, mostly black-backed gulls, screeched insanely as they were buffeted by a ferocious coastal wind that carried with it gritty specks of sand. The mouth of the Flaxbourne River was protected by an arc of rocks; the actual river was but a narrow channel that

A singleman's cottage is one of a number of buildings on Weld Cone that date to the Flaxbourne period.

might have been blasted out of the rock. On the south side of the river stood Weld Cone.

Narrow-eyed on account of the wind, I looked up at Weld Cone and recalled that Frederick Weld and Thomas Arnold had once climbed it together.

Thomas Arnold was the youngest son of Dr Thomas Arnold, headmaster of Rugby School in England, home of New Zealand's national sport. Young Thomas, whose eldest brother was the poet Matthew Arnold, visited Flaxbourne for three weeks in 1848 and, luckily for me, he frequently put pen to paper.

On the 4th October 1848 leaving Port Nicholson and launching out in the little cutter, the Petrel, which was navigated by two of Weld's men and himself, on the turbulent water outside, we had a grand view of the Kaikouras facing us across Cook Strait. We steered for Cape Campbell and then coasted along to Flaxbourne Cove, about eight miles [13 kilometres] to the southward. The station, a wooden building in two wings, with a kind of verandah connecting them, painted white, with stables, sheepyards etc., stood about a mile from the beach.

On the night (or rather morning) of the 16th October, between one and two a.m., the whole household was roused from sleep by the shock of an earthquake. I awoke and found myself being rocked violently from side to side in bed, like an infant in a cradle. The bottles in a loft above our heads kept up an insane dance and chatter; every timber in the house creaked, groaned and trembled; the dogs barked; and the shepherds (who slept in one wing of the house, Weld and I occupying the other) imagining the end of the world had come, rushed out of the house, and did not venture to return till daylight. Weld and I remained in the house but could not sleep. On Sunday, six days after the first shakes, we walked to the top of Weld Cone; seated on the narrow conical summit we gazed on the sublime appearance of the Kaikouras covered in snow. While we were thus intent there came a shock which distinctly made the top of the hills heave to and fro.

Looking across the Flaxbourne River to the exotic trees, drab in winter, that mark the site of Weld's homestead, Grassmere.

for the station; it had taken more than a year to build them all, and it would be the last time they used cob as a building material on Flaxbourne.

Evening came and went; dusk faded. At about 9.15 on both sides of Cook Strait the greatest earthquake – or rather series of earthquakes – ever recorded in New Zealand occurred. Such was the magnitude of the main earthquake (at least 8.0 on the Richter scale) that in places the land rose 2 metres. Wellington was devastated and the extensive swamplands in the lower Wairarapa were drained, destroying the breeding ground of Weld's hated mosquitoes.

At Flaxbourne anything built of cob or clay was flattened, including every one of the new cottages and much of the sheepyards and paddock fencing. Weld's homestead rocked like a boat in a big surf but somehow withstood it all.

The huge uplift of land reduced the depth of water in the lower, tidal reaches of the Flaxbourne River, buckling and reshaping the rocks at the rivermouth. No longer was it possible to bring a small vessel up the river or to use the deepish channel as a safe harbour. From this time until the subdivision in 1905 the station's woolclip was taken out by surfboat to coastal steamers.

As it turned out, this earthquake, perhaps of 7.0 or 7.5 magnitude, was merely an omen of worse to come.

The afternoon of 23 February 1855 had been pleasant enough at Flaxbourne: perhaps it was a little too humid, a little too still, a rather breathless sort of afternoon. Work had just finished on 16 cob cottages

Again I looked up at Weld Cone; again I let my eyes sweep over the narrow mouth of the Flaxbourne River and the craggy rocks that contained it. Then I turned my back on the boisterous sea and headed inland.

Beyond the site of Weld's first homestead on the Flaxbourne, perhaps 3 kilometres from the sea, I crossed a bridge over the river and came suddenly to a T-junction from which both roads led to State Highway 1. Close to the junction there were some old station buildings: part of a woolshed and yards, stables, a singleman's cottage, even the remains of a wagon. These buildings seemed to date to very early in the Flaxbourne story, but since 1905 they had stood on Weld Cone station.

The Butt family had won the ballot for this 630-hectare block on the true right of the river and it remained in their hands for a good many years. Today, however, Weld Cone station was owned by the Webby family. Ted and Vera and their son Nick ran a Merino halfbred flock where Weld's Grassmere homestead once stood. I called on them and asked if I could poke about the old station buildings; they had no objections.

In a dusty, cobwebbed part of a large woolshed my eyes were drawn to a sliding wooden door. On the door, stencilled in black like a woolbale, was a single word, a name that to me brought the past alive. The word was WELD. I gazed at the name for several long minutes and I wondered if the Webbys realised the significance of it – if they had noticed it there.

It was near these particular buildings that a second homestead was built on Flaxbourne in 1860. This more

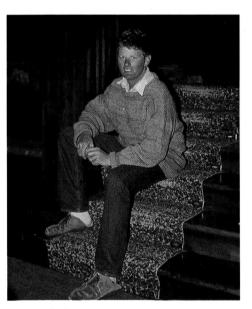

A grand place to grow up in: Lecester Murray in the family home.

or less coincided with Frederick Weld's return to New Zealand with his wife, and the two-storeyed homestead may have been seen as a more appropriate residence for Weld's wife when she visited from Brackenfield.

In any event, the new homestead was erected on the other side of the river from Grassmere. The block on which it stood became known as the Homestead block, and it went up for ballot in 1905 by that name. The lucky recipients of this nearly 1200-hectare slice of coastal country were a father and son, A.D. and A.F. Loe, who called their property The Homestead. It remained in the same family today. Frederick Loe's grandson Kevin took over the station in about 1979 and he and his wife Carol lived in a spacious homestead that dated to the mid-1920s.

Carol explained that they ran 3000 Corriedale sheep and 300 Angus cattle. The married couple on the place were Ross and Shirley Agnew, and they had been here even longer than Kevin and Carol. Recently both families had purchased between them a small adjoining coastal property called The Shirt, which was run separately and carried a Merino flock. Carol also told me that one section of the 1860s homestead was still in use: it had been incorporated into an attractive cottage – most likely a married couple's home – years ago.

Soon I was barrelling along State Highway 1 north of Ward, bound for today's Flaxbourne station, the name given to the Cape Campbell country the Cliffords had somehow managed to retain in 1905.

Ted and Nick (left) Webby on Weld Cone station.

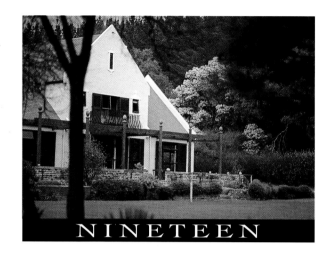

NINETEEN

FLAXBOURNE TODAY

Located between the mouth of the Awatere River and Cape Campbell, the lake named by Frederick Weld after his first homestead on Flaxbourne was more of a huge lagoon than anything else. To the Maori, however, the lake and neighbouring moa-hunter site were known as Kapara-te-hau, meaning "blown with the wind".

It was here, near Lake Grassmere, that in 1905 seven blocks of land, close to the Cape Campbell country the Cliffords retained, were created. Before the subdivision, the hilly Cape Campbell peninsula was known as the Hogget block, and it was an ideal location for the young male sheep to range free. On the flatlands near the lake a few buildings made up an out-station that was used by anyone wanting a bed while travelling north from the main Flaxbourne station area.

All in all the Cliffords did well by hanging on to the 5000-hectare Cape Campbell block; there was no finer country anywhere on the original Flaxbourne run. They retained Everade Weld as manager of the new Flaxbourne and built a whole new station complex.

It was, however, only a matter of a few years before the Cliffords decided to sell the little they retained of the once massive station. They auctioned off three farm-sized blocks north of Lake Elterwater in 1911, and a

The ivy-clad dairy is one of a number of buildings that date from the time of the new Flaxbourne station complex.

Part of the original 1860s farmhouse, known as The Homestead, still stands on the Loes' station.

year later six grazing blocks on the peninsula went the same way.

All that was left was the jewel in the crown: the 1200-hectare homestead block, which was purchased by Everade Weld. The son of Frederick Weld took a great interest in local affairs and he retained Flaxbourne until his death in 1956 at the age of 88. Life in New Zealand had been good to this Englishman.

The station now passed into the hands of Weld's only child, Constance Mary, who that same year had married Simon Scrope and was living in England. Flaxbourne was run by a succession of managers until Constance died and the station came into the hands of her two daughters – one of whom, Cecily, came out to Flaxbourne with her husband in 1975.

It was in 1967 that Cecily Scrope had met Robin Petre, who, incredibly, was related to the Henry Petre who was a part of the original Wharekaka venture of 1844.

I met Cecily and Robin at today's Flaxbourne station. "You know," I said, turning to Robin, "it is a truly amazing coincidence."

With a chuckle Robin Petre said, "Yes, isn't it."

Even though he was seated and relaxed, there was still a strong military bearing about this 54-year-old Briton; I wasn't surprised to learn that he'd spent 14 years in the British Army. There was no point in asking him his rank: he was clearly officer material from the day he was born.

"You must have known very little about sheep when you came here," I said to Robin.

"No, nothing at all, to be honest," he replied with disarming frankness. "But," he added in an authoritative tone, "one had to learn pretty quickly."

"Robin was brought up on a very large estate," Cecily said in his defence. "Country life wasn't entirely foreign."

Robin had found himself in much the same situation as Frederick Weld, Alphonso Clifford and George Lovegrove when they first arrived in New Zealand, and they all learnt pretty quickly. One way or another those of British stock generally made out.

Today they ran 3500 Corriedale sheep and 200 Angus cattle on Flaxbourne's further reduced 1000 hectares. A married couple, Peter and Betty Marshall, lived at the station too; I gathered Peter was a jack of all trades – and probably master of more than one.

When Cecily and Robin first arrived in 1975 they lived in the homestead that Everade Weld had resided in for so many years. Basically, the homestead had originated from a cluster of musterers' cottages from the days when this was the Hogget block. Using Australian jarrah as his main building timber, Weld had cleverly joined them all together to form a sprawling mansion.

FLAXBOURNE

Flaxbourne was the first great South Island sheep run. It was established in 1847 by Charles Clifford and Frederick Weld, on land leased from Te Puaha, a Ngati Toa Chief. Clifford shipped some 3000 sheep from Sydney to Port Underwood in July 1847; they were driven to Flaxbourne in August. At its peak in 1879 the run consisted of 72,000 acres carrying 60,000 sheep In 1905 the Government purchased 45,000 acres for subdivision into 80 farms. The remaining land was cut up in 1913.

The Petres' last night in the homestead was 5 February 1993. Cecily recalled that a little after two o'clock in the morning her light slumber was disturbed. She sat up in bed, not quite fully awake, puzzled: what had awoken her?

Outside a powerful nor'-wester was blowing, shaking the branches of the many exotic trees that Everade Weld had planted. But it wasn't the wind, it was something else, something strange. The sound seemed to come from the kitchen, where their five Cavalier King Charles spaniels slept. Was one of them in distress?

Cecily slipped out of bed, being careful not to disturb Robin. Suddenly the source of the strange noise was unmistakable – it was the roar of an inferno. The whole downstairs floor had exploded into leaping flames, and the heat was intense.

Frantically Cecily fled back to the master bedroom and, heart pounding, she shook Robin awake.

"Fire!" she screamed at him.

Clad in only their night garments, Cecily and Robin managed to rescue four of their five precious dogs before being beaten back by the heat and smoke. The homestead was gutted, and everything, from valuable paintings and antiques to irreplaceable family mementoes, destroyed.

It was generally believed that an electrical fault in a hot-water cylinder had started the fire. Whatever the cause, this much was certain: once the bone-dry jarrah was alight it had, in Cecily's words, "gone up like a rocket". Which was precisely what such trees did when engulfed in an Australian bush fire.

From the ashes of Everade Weld's grand old mansion had risen today's Flaxbourne homestead. With the architectural inspiration of Sir Michael Fowler and the craftsmanship of Ian Barnes, this 325-square-metre dwelling was by any standards a magnificent home.

For Cecily and Robin Petre, linked by their families' past as well as their marriage vows, the destruction of the homestead did not mark the end of a proud history so much as the beginning of another chapter. I could not help but agree with the sentiments of my charming hosts.

As we took a stroll around the garden we were accompanied by the four spaniels that had survived the fire. They had given me a great reception when I had arrived: much tail thumping, much good-natured grinning. Being well-bred creatures, however, they had settled down quietly while we talked over tea. I imagined that Cecily and Robin, who treasured their dogs in the way that only the English do, still numbered them as five rather than four.

The site of the original Flaxbourne station was marked by a New Zealand Historic Places Trust noticeboard on the edge of the narrow road to Ward Beach, close to the old woolshed on Weld Cone station.

Many of those who had been associated with the station were present at the unveiling on 8 September 1963. Among them was 90-year-old Alf Loe of nearby The Homestead station, a man who had actually known George Lovegrove. Two representatives from the Clifford and Weld families were there: Cecily Scrope and Mrs George McDonald of Christchurch, a granddaughter of Sir Charles Clifford. From his home in Dorset, England, Lieutenant Colonel H.G. Weld, MC, the only son of Sir Frederick Weld's eldest son, sent a message, part of which read, "From small beginnings, such as Flaxbourne, had risen a nation famed all over the world for the skill of its pastoralists and the superb quality of its fighting men."

All in all, a fitting way, I think, to bring the saga of the first great sheep station in the South Island to a close.

At today's Flaxbourne: Robin and Cecily Petre.

The present-day homestead at Flaxbourne.

Long Journey's
End

As all things surely must, the trilogy of *Station Country* books has come to a close. By no stretch of the imagination are these books meant to be definitive works – rather, I have strived through words and pictures to convey the essence of station life in this country: how it began, how it developed, and how it shapes up today.

I have visited many stations throughout the land to gather material. Between 1990 and 1996 I made four trips to the North Island, and my South Island forays numbered many more than that. In both islands I have seen country that was new to me. What I saw, gazing sometimes in wonder, often in delight, frequently in frustration because the photographic light was poor, only confirmed what I already knew – that New Zealand is a country of many extremes and many moods, and that those of us who have seen it at first hand are truly blessed.

There are a good many stations in this country that would have proven equally rewarding to write about as those I have included. There are well in excess of 300 properties in the South Island classed as high-country runs, and a great many more stations than that in the North Island. I simply could not cover them all.

The people I have come into contact with on stations have, in the main, gone right out of their way to assist me. In many instances it went far beyond what I had any right to expect. Words cannot express how I feel about such generosity of spirit.

I consider the people who live and work on stations to be especially fortunate. It is a good way of life, one that will carry on despite the expansion of dairying, forestry and the increasing number of lifestyle blocks. While sheep numbers have dropped in recent years, I find it impossible to envisage a New Zealand where sheep do not greatly out-number the human population.

It has been my extreme good fortune to have worked on the Station Country trilogy, and I regard writing them as a highlight of my career. I will remember the experience with deep pleasure for the rest of my life.

First light in the Maniototo.

REFERENCES

Acland, L.G.D., *The Early Canterbury Runs*, Whitcombe & Tombs, Christchurch, 1930/1975.

Aubrey, M., *Omarama: Place of Light,* New Zealand Official Project, 1978.

Beattie, H., *Early Runholding in Otago*, self-published, 1947.

Beattie, H., *The Southern Runs*, Gore Historical Society, 1949.

Belich, J., *The New Zealand Wars*, Penguin, Auckland, 1988.

Brailsford, B., & Mitchell, D., *The Kingston Flyer*, Footrot Press, Christchurch, 1986.

Complete Dispersal of Station Bred Horses, Elders Pastoral Sales Booklet (Ihungia), 1996.

Cowan, C., *Down the Years in the Maniototo*, Otago Centennial Historical Publications, 1948.

Crawford, S.C., *Sheep and Sheepmen of Canterbury*, Simpson & Williams, Christchurch, 1949.

Creswell, D., *Early New Zealand Families*, Whitcombe & Tombs, Christchurch, 1956.

Cumberland, K.B., *Landmarks*, Readers Digest, Sydney, 1981.

Duncan, A.H. *The Wakatipians*, Lakes District Centennial Museum, 1964.

Fearon, K.J., *Te Wharau*, Netherton Grange Publications, Masterton, undated.

Flaxbourne-Kekerengu, Marlborough Historical Society, 1972.

Gilkison, R., *Eary Days in Central Otago*, Otago Daily Times/Witness Newspapers, Dunedin, 1930.

Graham, J., *Frederick Weld*, Auckland University Press/Oxford University Press, 1969.

Grigg, S.E., *A Southern Gentry*, A.H. & A.W. Reed, Wellington, 1980.

Harris, R., *Otairi 1881–1981*, Otairi station/Dunmore Press, Palmerston North, 1986.

"High country magic", *Southland Times*, 13 April 1996.

Kennington, A.L., *The Awatere*, Marlborough County Council, 1978.

"Lambs vanish from parched peninsula", "Magic days on isle of sheep and crays",
   "Low tide puts stop to shearing on Portland", *New Zealand Farmer*, 11 January 1995.

"Loving memories of country days", *Daily Telegraph* (Napier), 29 January 1982.

McCaskill, L.W., *Molesworth*, A.H. & A.W. Reed, Wellington, 1969.

MacGregor, M. *Early Stations of Hawke's Bay*, A.H. & A.W. Reed, Wellington, 1980.

MacGregor Redwood, M., *A Dog's Life*, A.H. & A.W. Reed, Wellington, 1980.

Mackenzie, F., *The Sparkling Waters of Whakatipu*, A.H. & A.W. Reed, Wellington, 1947.

Miller, F.W.G., *Golden Days of Lake County*, Whitcombe & Tombs, Christchurch, 1949.

Neave, E. & M., *The Land of Munros, Merinos & Matagouri*, self-published, Kurow, 1980.

Newton, P., *Big Country of the North Island*, A.H. & A.W. Reed, Wellington, 1969.

Newton, P., *Big Country of the South Island*, A.H. & A.W. Reed, Wellington, 1973.

Newton, P., *In the Wake of the Axe*, A.H. & A.W. Reed, Wellington, 1972.

Newton, P., *Sixty Thousand on the Hoof*, A.H. & A.W. Reed, Wellington, 1975.

New Zealand Home Collection, NZ Master Builders Federation, 1995–96.

Pinney, R., *Early Canterbury Runs*, A.H. & A.W. Reed, Wellington, 1971.

Pinney, R., *Early Northern Otago Runs*, Collins, Auckland, 1981.

"Tangihau station – strong responsive country", *New Zealand Farmer*, 8 December 1983.

Thornton, G.C., *The New Zealand Heritage of Farm Buildings*, Reed Methuen, Auckland, 1986.

Vance, W., *High Endeavour*, A.H. & A.W. Reed, Wellington, 1965.

Ward, L.E., *Early Wellington*, Whitcombe & Tombs, Christchurch, 1928.

Wheeler, C., *Historical Sheep Stations of New Zealand*, Beckett, Auckland, 1969.

Wilson, E., *The Story of Captain Howell and his Family*, self-published, 1976.

Wises New Zealand Guide, Wises, Auckland, 1989

PHOTOGRAPHIC NOTES

To take the photographs for the *Station Country* books I used two Nikon F301 camera bodies and Nikkor lenses: 35-millimetre 1:1.2, 85-millimetre 1:1.2, 135-millimetre 1:1.28, 200-millimetre 1:1.4 and 300-millimetre 1:4.5

I used a simple skylight filter to protect the lenses rather than to improve the quality of the photograph. The other filter I used was a polarising filter, to darken too-light sky or water or to create something special out of the commonplace.

Whenever possible I used a Hanimex HX-V100 tripod; failing that, I supported the camera on a fencepost, a rock, whatever. I only took a photograph in a totally hand-held position as a last resort.

Films used were Ektachrome 100 Professional Plus, Fujichrome lOOD, and Fujichrome Provia 100.

My advice to any budding professional photographer is to take plenty of photographs. The cost of film and processing it is relatively cheap – it is the getting there and the time involved that is expensive.